INTERNATIONAL DEVELOPMENT IN FOCUS

Budget Rigidity in Latin America and the Caribbean

Causes, Consequences, and Policy Implications

SANTIAGO HERRERA AND EDUARDO OLABERRIA

Contents

Boxes

Figures

Tables

Acknowledgments

This report was prepared by co-task team leaders Santiago Herrera (lead economist) and Eduardo Olaberria (senior economist) in the Macro-Fiscal unit of the Macroeconomics, Trade and Investment Global Practice, with the help of Ercio Muñoz (consultant). It is based on a collection of technical papers prepared for the Latin America and the Caribbean Regional Study on budget rigidities by a team including Julio Velasco (economist), Jürgen von Hagen (consultant), Juan Carlos Echeverry (consultant), Fernando Lorenzo (consultant), Jose Pacheco (consultant), Santiago Herrera, Ercio Muñoz, and Eduardo Olaberria. Peer reviewers were Fernando Blanco, Fernando Im, and Steven Pennings.

The team gratefully acknowledges the valuable collaboration and support of Carlos Vegh, Elena Ianchovichina, and Guillermo Vuletin. The authors also acknowledge comments on earlier versions of the background technical papers by Jorge Araujo, Fernando Blanco, Cristina Savescu, Daniel Riera-Crichton, and Franziska Lieselotte Ohnsorge, and comments on earlier drafts by Sebastian Eckardt, Cesar Calderon, and Pablo Saavedra.

About the Authors

Santiago Herrera is a lead economist who has worked in the Macroeconomics, Trade and Investment Global Practice in the Latin America and the Caribbean, Middle East and North Africa, and Sub-Saharan Africa regions at the World Bank. Before joining the World Bank, he was the Director of the National Budget and Deputy Minister of Finance in Colombia. He pursued PhD studies at Columbia University in New York City.

Eduardo Olaberria is a senior economist in the Macroeconomics, Trade and Investment Global Practice at the World Bank. Previously, he was senior economist in the Department of Economics of the Organisation for Economic Co-operation and Development. He has also worked at the Central Bank of Chile, the Ministry of Finance of Argentina, and the research department of the Inter-American Development Bank. His research interests include macroeconomics, international finance, and fiscal policy. He has published a dozen articles in scientific journals and specialized books. He has an MA and PhD in economics from Universidad Torcuato di Tella and the University of Maryland, respectively.

Executive Summary

Many Latin American countries are facing daunting fiscal challenges following a considerable surge in debt–to–gross domestic product (GDP) ratios in recent years. Estimates of fiscal gaps suggest that substantial fiscal tightening will be needed in nearly all countries to stabilize their public debts (Vegh et al. 2018). Although strong growth can help address these challenges, the bulk of the consolidation will require structural reforms to spending and revenue to stabilize and possibly reduce debt-to-GDP ratios. However, policy makers claim that their ability to adjust is constrained by a high degree of budget rigidity, as a large share of public spending is difficult to cut for political economy or structural reasons.

Budget rigidities are institutional, legal, contractual, or other constraints that limit the ability of the government to change the size and structure of the public budget, at least in the short term. They originate as the result of the following factors:

- Economic growth, which imposes natural trends on the wage level and is associated with the larger size of the public sector
- Demographic factors such as aging of the population, which induces inertia on pension payments
- Distributional conflicts in the context of budget opacity and fragmentation
- External constraints in the form of rules that predetermine the level or share of certain types of expenditure
- The budget's dual role as a legal instrument for accountability and as a functional tool to manage public spending levels and composition.

In recent years, budget rigidities have become more relevant to policy makers in the region because tools for fiscal adjustment used in the past are no longer available. With lower inflation, governments have lost a revenue source and a mechanism to reduce in real terms nominal debt and other contracts. Consequently, countries have relied more on cutting public investment, which is the more flexible component of public spending, than on addressing budget rigidities. Vegh et al. (2018) find that, before 2007, reductions in public investment represented 55 percent of typical fiscal adjustments; after 2007, this figure grew to 79 percent. However, cutting public investment can be costly in the long run because it can have large negative impacts on economic growth. Lower GDP growth can cause further deterioration of the fiscal situation, requiring a larger adjustment down the road. Furthermore, public investment levels in the region are already meager. Thus, governments need to act now by tackling the more rigid components of spending.

Despite being a frequent complaint of policy makers, the issue of how rigid spending affects fiscal performance has largely been ignored by the literature, mostly because of the lack of adequate measures of rigidity that track its prevalence over time and allow cross-country comparisons. This report helps close this gap by introducing a new measure of spending rigidity that can be applied to a large set of countries across time. This new measure focuses on the categories of public spending that are naturally inflexible—such as wages, pensions, and debt service—and separates them into two components—a structural component and a nonstructural one. The structural component is determined by economic, demographic, and institutional fundamentals, while the nonstructural component is determined by short-run transitory or political factors associated with business or political cycles. The degree of rigidity of spending is then proxied by the ratio of structural spending to total spending. A higher value of the ratio indicates that spending is driven mostly by structural factors, implying that policy makers in this situation would find it more difficult to adjust public spending.

Calculating this new measure for 120 countries for the years 2000–17 produces the following stylized facts:

- First, rigidity is not an exclusive phenomenon of Latin America and the Caribbean (LAC); other regions, such as Europe and Central Asia (ECA) and the Middle East and North Africa (MENA), as well as high-income countries belonging to the Organisation for Economic Co-operation and Development (OECD), have higher levels of rigid expenditures than LAC. As a percentage of total spending, the LAC regional average of rigid spending is below 70 percent, lower than that in ECA or MENA (see chapter 3 for more details). Within LAC, there is significant heterogeneity; the rigid component of spending is higher in Argentina, Bolivia, Brazil, and Jamaica than in other countries.[1]

- Second, expenditure rigidity in LAC seems to be lower than estimated in previous analyses, indicating that there is more room for policy action than is suggested by measures found in earlier literature. Although previous studies show rigidity levels in excess of 90 percent of total spending for many countries, our estimates are in the range of 70 percent. Although this is still a significant portion of spending, it is 25 percent lower, allowing room for fiscal policy discretion.

- Third, the sources of rigidity are heterogeneous and vary by country. Interest payments are a major source of rigidity in Barbados, Brazil, Colombia, Costa Rica, and Jamaica, while in other countries the wage bill is the major source of rigidity. For instance, the structural component of the wage bill is highest in Colombia and Panama, leaving less room to maneuver than in Argentina, Bolivia, Ecuador, and Honduras, where the structural factors account for a lower percentage of wage bill spending. Finally, pension payments are a larger source of rigidity in Chile, Panama, and Peru, in which almost 100 percent of spending on pension payments is driven by structural factors, than in Argentina, Brazil, Ecuador, Nicaragua, and Uruguay, in which there is greater scope for policy action.

The report investigates how budget rigidities affect fiscal performance across countries. The following findings emerge from the report:

- Higher rigidity is associated with higher spending levels, higher tax rates, higher public debt, and lower efficiency of public spending.
- In the long run, rigidity has pervasive effects on sustainability; models show that during bad times, the net worth of the government is significantly impaired when spending is more rigid.
- Rigidity has short-run impacts on outcomes and policy making. The main impact is that rigidity increases the country's financing needs and reduces the probability of the country starting a fiscal adjustment.
- Rigidity can, notwithstanding, help reduce the procyclical behavior of fiscal policy typically found in developing countries. The effect is asymmetric, meaning that it slows spending during a boom more than it stops spending during a contraction.

In the long term, policy makers need to reinforce the battle against budget rigidities to contain the sources of rigidity discussed in this report. The main elements of such a strategy should include the following:

- Continuing and deepening the pension reform process, by increasing the retirement age and facilitating private sector participation in the pension funds sector;
- Ensuring that fiscal institutions that promote medium-term fiscal planning incorporate the costs of any wage increases over time;
- Delegating decisions on long-term budget composition matters, such as the wage bill over the long run, to technical fiscal councils;
- Increasing transparency in the budget to reduce the need for spending floors or spending rules to ensure allocation of resources to specific activities;
- Reducing budget fragmentation, given that the complete picture of public resource allocation and distribution allows for a more expedient budget approval process that can change as circumstances change;
- Limiting earmarking and providing exit clauses to existing constitutional spending mandates. The policy maker should have discretion in the case of fiscal imbalances.

NOTE

1. Rigid spending is the sum of the structural components of the wage bill and pension payments, plus interest payments.

REFERENCE

Vegh, Carlos, Guillermo Vuletin, Daniel Riera-Crichton, Diego Friedheim, Luis Morano, and José Andrée Camarana. 2018. *Fiscal Adjustment in Latin America and the Caribbean: Short-Run Pain, Long-Run Gain?* LAC Semiannual Report. Washington, DC: World Bank Group.

Abbreviations

CPB   Central Planning Bureau
EAP   East Asia and Pacific
ECA   Europe and Central Asia
GDP   gross domestic product
LAC   Latin America and the Caribbean
MENA   Middle East and North Africa
OECD   Organisation for Economic Co-operation and Development
SNG   subnational government
SSA   Sub-Saharan Africa

1 Introduction

Many countries in Latin America are facing daunting fiscal challenges following a substantial surge in debt–to–gross domestic product (GDP) ratios during recent years (figure 1.1). Estimates of fiscal gaps suggest that sustained fiscal tightening will be needed in nearly all countries in Latin America and the Caribbean (LAC) to bring debt down to prudent levels (Vegh et al. 2018). Furthermore, with rising volatility in world financial markets, public debt sustainability will become a major concern in many countries in the region, obliging more governments to generate high primary surpluses at a time when growth prospects are being revised downward.

Governments in LAC seem unable to initiate fiscal consolidation, in contrast with other regions. Although Organisation for Economic Co-operation and Development countries have already gone through successful fiscal consolidation processes, in Latin America, fiscal deficits have increased (figure 1.2). A significant portion of the increase in fiscal deficits in South America can be explained by higher spending levels. Additionally, fiscal pressures continue to build because of population aging (in some cases) and the need to invest in human and physical capital to foster long-term growth.

Budget rigidities are often cited as a reason for slow progress with fiscal adjustment in Latin America. Policy makers in the region argue that their ability to carry out large fiscal adjustments is constrained by institutional, legal, contractual, or other constraints that constitute budget rigidities and limit the ability of the government to change the size and structure of the public budget, at least in the short term. Several budget components are naturally inflexible, including wages, pensions, and debt service. But there are other inflexibilities that are rooted in the constitution, laws, or decrees, such as provisions that earmark revenues, set minimum spending requirements, or link spending to the evolution of macroeconomic variables such as inflation, growth, or unemployment.

The issue of budget rigidities is not limited to Latin America. Policy makers all over the world complain about budget rigidities and express concerns about their growth and adverse effects on fiscal performance. Schick (2007) recognizes a general tendency of weakening budget control and of budgets being ruled by "force majeure." Assuming, as a first approximation, that government transfers, the wage bill, and interest spending are "rigid," then the share of rigid items

FIGURE 1.1

Rise in debt-to-GDP ratios in Latin America, 2012 and 2017

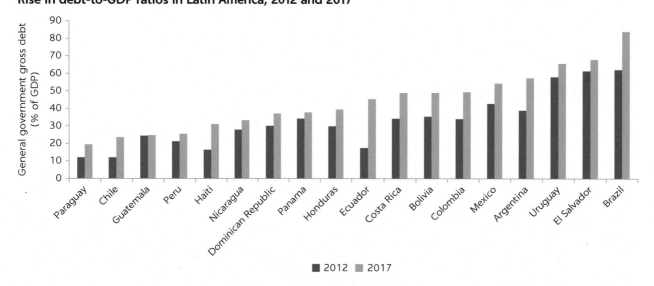

Source: International Monetary Fund 2018.
Note: GDP = gross domestic product.

FIGURE 1.2

General government net lending/borrowing, 2009–18

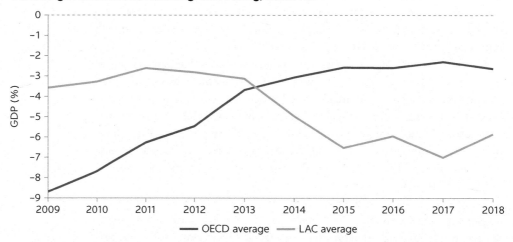

Source: International Monetary Fund 2019.
Note: GDP = gross domestic product; LAC = Latin America and the Caribbean; OECD = Organisation for Economic Co-operation and Development.

in total government spending in 2014 was 88 percent, on average, in European Union countries, 89 percent in the United States, and 80 percent in Japan (von Hagen and Chen 2019).

Despite being a frequent complaint of policy makers, the issue of how budget rigidities affect fiscal performance has remained largely ignored by the literature. Although there is plentiful anecdotal evidence on how rigid spending can hinder sound policies, there has been little empirical work on the subject. Most of the existing studies focus on quantifying the extent of rigidities in specific countries for a limited time (for example, Echeverry, Bonilla, and Moya 2006; Cetrángolo,

Jiménez, and del Castillo 2009; Mattina and Gunnarsson 2007). These results show that budget rigidities in terms of the share of total spending or GDP differ widely across countries in Latin America and the Caribbean, from mid-60 percent in Chile to more than 90 percent in Brazil, Colombia, and Costa Rica. Few studies include cross-country comparisons, and the methodologies for the calculation of budget rigidities vary across countries. The centrality of the issue for fiscal policy and the limited existing analysis underscore the need for broader quantifications of spending rigidities and their impact on fiscal outcomes.

This report seeks to help close this gap in the literature by assessing budget rigidities and their effects on the fiscal performance of countries. Chapter 2 reviews the different definitions and sources of budget rigidities identified in the literature. Chapter 3 proposes new, simple measures of budget rigidities that allow for cross-country statistical analysis over time. Chapter 4 examines how rigidities influence fiscal performance and their policy implications for the sustainability of public finance, the ability of government to perform fiscal adjustments, the cyclicality of fiscal policy management, and the efficiency of public spending. Chapter 5 provides a conclusion.

REFERENCES

Cetrángolo, Oscar, Juan Pablo Jiménez, and Ramiro Ruiz del Castillo. 2009. "Rigideces y Espacios Fiscales en America Latina." Serie Documento de Proyecto 269, Economic Commission for Latin America and the Caribbean (ECLAC), Santiago, Chile.

Echeverry, Juan Carlos, Jorge Alexander Bonilla, and Andres Moya. 2006. "Rigideces institucionales y flexibilidad presupuestaria: Los casos de Argentina, Colombia, México y Perú." Documento CEDE 2006-33, Universidad de los Andes, Bogotá, Colombia.

International Monetary Fund. 2018. World Economic Outlook database, October. https://www.imf.org/en/Publications/SPROLLs/world-economic-outlook-databases#sort=%40imfdate%20descending.

———. 2019. World Economic Outlook database, April. https://www.imf.org/en/Publications/SPROLLs/world-economic-outlook-databases#sort=%40imfdate%20descending

Mattina, Todd, and Victoria Gunnarsson. 2007. "Budget Rigidity and Expenditure Efficiency in Slovenia." IMF Working Paper WP/07/131, International Monetary Fund, Washington, DC.

Schick, Allen. 2007. "Off-Budget Expenditure: An Economic and Political Framework." *OECD Journal of Budgeting* 7 (3): 1–32.

Vegh, Carlos, Guillermo Vuletin, Daniel Riera-Crichton, Diego Friedheim, Luis Morano, and José Andrée Camarana. 2018. *Fiscal Adjustment in Latin America and the Caribbean: Short-Run Pain, Long-Run Gain?* LAC Semiannual Report. Washington, DC: World Bank Group.

von Hagen, Jurgen, and Chen. 2019. "Budget Rigidities and Fiscal Performance in Latin America and the Caribbean." Background Report for Regional Study on Budget Rigidities in Latin America, unpublished paper, World Bank, Washington, DC.

2 Definition, Origins, and Sources of Budget Rigidities

Among a variety of definitions of budget rigidities in the academic literature, the most useful ones highlight that rigidity has a time dimension imposed by "institutional restrictions that limit the ability to modify the level or structure of the government budget within a certain period of time"(Echeverry, Bonilla, and Moya 2006, 7; Cetrángolo, Jiménez, and Ruiz del Castillo 2010). These restrictions can result from contractual obligations, such as public sector wage agreements, interest payments on public debt, or the financing of large investment projects extending over several years. In addition, they can be the result of legal or other formal actions limiting discretionary government authority to make changes to the budget, such as the protection of certain types of expenditures by constitutional or other legal provisions. Expenditures that are mandated by laws outside the budget process, such as entitlements and social security benefits, are a further source of rigidities. Finally, rigidities can stem from institutional weaknesses of the budget process, such as when actors in this process are unable to reach agreements or when the scope of government action is limited by outside institutional actors, such as courts.

The kinds of rigidities that raise concerns for fiscal performance are those that prevent governments from adjusting the budget over a period of one to three years. This may occur during periods of macroeconomic volatility or mounting fiscal pressures. Thus, budget items can be considered rigid when the government cannot adjust them significantly within one to three years.

Rigidity is caused partly by the nature of public budgets, which emerge from a political process involving many different actors from all branches of government. The budget serves to implement and execute government policies, the principles and rules of which are defined outside the budget process. If a budget is overly rigid, the budget process cannot fulfill its constitutional role as the arena in which political competition for fiscal resources is played out. As a result, political actors and interest groups seek out and find new ways of precommitting government expenditures outside the budget process. Thus, budget rigidities develop their own dynamics, which are reflected in the fact that their importance has grown considerably in Latin America and the Caribbean and elsewhere over time.

However, budgetary rigidities can be useful and desirable to achieve certain long-term goals in an uncertain environment. Many government policies pursue long-term goals and their success depends on the credibility of the government's commitment to sustain these policies over long time horizons. For example, when the central government makes grants to subnational governments to enable them to finance infrastructure investment or health and education programs, the subnational governments will use these funds for the intended purposes only if they can expect to receive the transfers over a long period of time. Citizens will be reluctant to engage in long-term education programs if there is a significant risk that the programs will stop for financial reasons before they can be completed, leaving them with no useful outcome.

But excessive rigidity can also be detrimental for the performance of public finance if the government cannot respond to changing needs. Rigidity can prevent the government from varying the level or composition of public spending in response to changing priorities or needs, and thus reduce the effectiveness of public policies. For example, a central government forced to maintain transfers for local infrastructure to subnational governments is likely to end up financing local projects with low returns, and possibly miss the opportunity to finance more productive projects. The greater the specificity of the purpose for such transfers, the greater the rigidities and their negative impact. Block grants, or regular spending reviews, which some countries have introduced as part of their budget processes, might be ways to avoid such inefficiencies.

STRUCTURAL SOURCES OF BUDGET RIGIDITIES

Budget rigidities can arise from different sources that can occur simultaneously and interact. They may be the result of structural developments of the economy; of characteristics of the budget process; or of politico-economic forces and developments. When these different factors occur simultaneously and interact, the problem of rigidities becomes more complex.

Demographic changes

One source of budget rigidity is long-term demographic change, which determines trends in public finance in ways that are difficult to change. One of the greatest challenges for public finance comes from dramatic demographic changes around the world. As the population of a country increases, so does the demand for public services. And as the population ages, the pressure on public finance increases as well (figure 2.1).

The pressure on public finance from the rising share of the elderly in the population occurs for several reasons. There is a rising share of people entitled to public pensions and a declining share of people who actively participate in the workforce and contribute to public pension schemes. The resulting financial squeeze of the public pension system calls into question the sustainability of public pension systems in the region, most of which are pay-as-you-go and are already severely underfunded. The fiscal consequences of an aging population also affect health spending, including the demand for elderly care and associated health care costs, which tend to escalate with age. Furthermore, an aging population requires responses in many areas of public policy, not just in the design of public pension and health systems.

Public wage dynamics

Another source of rigidity comes from the dynamics of public wages. The wage level increases with the level of wealth of the country, as noted by

FIGURE 2.1

Old age-dependency ratio and social security spending across the world

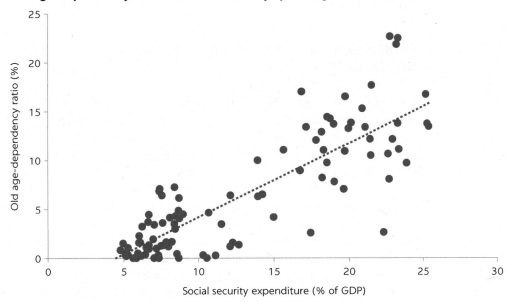

Sources: Calculations based on International Monetary Fund (2019) data and World Bank staff estimates.
Note: GDP = gross domestic product.

FIGURE 2.2

Public sector wages and GDP per capita, 1980–2016

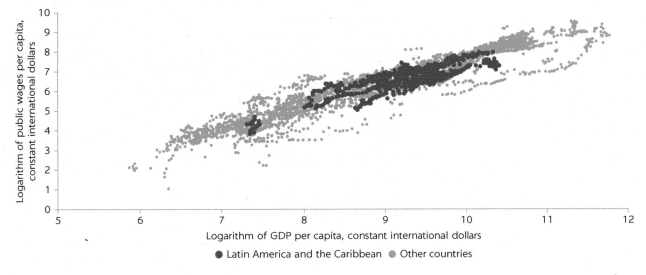

● Latin America and the Caribbean ● Other countries

Source: Herrera and Velasco 2019.
Note: GDP = gross domestic product.

development economists (Balassa 1964; Samuelson 1964; Bhagwati 1984). The Balassa-Samuelson hypothesis explains wage differentials across countries with different levels of productivity, which translate into higher wages in wealthier countries, because they have higher productivity levels. The Bhagwati model explains wage differentials across countries on the basis of factor endowment differences, with those with higher capital-to-labor ratios having higher wages.

Hence, wages tend to increase with the level of development of the country. If public sector wages are linked to private sector remuneration, these should also increase with the country's income level (figure 2.2).[1] Therefore, the portion of the budget dedicated to wages tends to increase as the country's income level rises.

ECONOMIC DEVELOPMENT AND THE SIZE OF GOVERNMENT

Long-run economic growth is typically coupled with even faster growth of the public sector than that of the economy. This well-known fact is known as Wagner's Law in public finance. Theories explaining the size of government generally are based on interactions between the citizen and the state and fall into two categories: theories that explain growth based on citizens' demand for public services, and theories that promote the idea that government inefficiencies are imposed on citizens by government bureaucrats (Garret and Rhine 2006). In democratic settings, in which the government responds to citizen preferences, it suggests positive income elasticity of demand (that is, demand increases as income increases) for public goods and government services in areas such as education, health, infrastructure, and provision of insurance against economic hardship.

The state's role in protecting citizens against economic hardship has been articulated by Dani Rodrik (2000), who developed a model in which the state insures citizens against undiversifiable external shocks via public employment. The more exposed the country is to external shocks, the higher public employment will be. Rodrik's model can be extended to examine the size of overall government spending as a mechanism to protect citizens against undiversifiable exposure to external risk (von Hagen and Chen 2019). The results suggest that the relative size of government desired by citizens can be explained by the degree of openness and the volatility of shocks affecting the economy. For instance, if a country faces volatile terms of trade, or swings in the demand for exports, the country will mitigate the risk through larger spending. A large government sector serves as a buffer against such shocks.

POLITICAL ECONOMY AND RIGIDITIES RESULTING FROM INSTITUTIONAL WEAKNESSES

The budget process provides the framework for the distributional conflicts over public resources that characterize fiscal policy. Fiscal policy involves competition between different groups in society and their representatives for tax revenues to be spent on projects that benefit them or their constituencies. The budget process is the constitutional locus where such conflicts over public resources are played out. Its role is to provide a framework in which all competing claims on public funds are manifested, confronted, and reconciled with each other. The budget process is shaped by budgeting institutions, which are defined generally as the collection of formal and informal rules and principles governing the budget process within the executive and the legislative branches of government.

Echeverry, Fergusson, and Querubin (2005) and Cetrángolo, Jiménez, and Ruiz del Castillo (2010) argue that most budget rigidities are the result of distributional conflicts between different interest groups or social classes within a country, but this depends on the design of the budget process. Distributional conflicts per se do not necessarily lead to rigidities—they do if the budget process is ill designed and does not enable the relevant political actors to make timely decisions. This may occur in several dimensions: fragmentation opacity of the budget process, the existence of external constraints, and an excessively legalistic approach to budgeting.

FRAGMENTATION OF THE BUDGET PROCESS

Budget rigidities can arise from excessive fragmentation of the budget process, which results in the inability of decision makers to effectively adjust the budget to changing political goals and economic and social circumstances. One dimension of fragmentation concerns the budget itself. To present all relevant trade-offs between different areas and goals of government policy, the budget should be presented in a comprehensive and unified document. When budgets are spread over different documents, each covering only parts of government expenditures, negotiations become more complicated, and some parts of the budget can be effectively shielded from political competition.

A factor that aggravates this problem is off-budget expenditures—expenditures not accounted for at all in the budget law. Off-budget expenditures may be funded by earmarked revenues or special levies on those benefiting from them, which then create off-budget funds. Decisions regarding off-budget expenditures are taken out of the context of government budgeting, and this creates procedural rigidities because these expenditures cannot be changed within the official budget process. Furthermore, off-budget expenditures and their funding are often governed by special boards, including representatives of the presumed beneficiaries, such as in the context of health or education programs. This creates new arenas of political conflict separated from the budget process.

OPACITY OF THE BUDGET PROCESS

Rigidities may arise as a mechanism to reduce negotiation costs in an imperfect information setting. The approval of the budget is a repeated bargaining situation between the executive and legislative branches of government, or between political parties. This bargaining occurs in a setting of imperfect and asymmetric information. The parties in the negotiation do not know with certainty the preferences of the other groups and do not know the costs of accepting a compromise. Lengthy bargaining becomes a way of discovering this information. To avoid these costs on a yearly basis, resource allocations may be decided by spending rules, which distribute resources across society or interest groups.

Some governments have put measures in place to increase the transparency of budget assessments. In the Netherlands, the Dutch Central Planning Bureau (CPB), an independent economic research institute, is charged with presenting an assessment of the government's annual budget proposal. In Dutch elections, opposition parties present their economic and fiscal programs to the CPB, which publishes an evaluation of their economic and fiscal consequences. Building on that example, European Union legislation now requires all countries belonging to the euro area to have independent fiscal councils. One of the official tasks of the fiscal councils is to approve the government's macroeconomic budget forecast and budget proposal.

EXTERNAL CONSTRAINTS ON BUDGETARY DECISIONS

External constraints on budgetary decisions are rules that predetermine the level or share of certain types of expenditures. The constraints work either through fixing expenditures or tying them to developments outside of the budget process. A prime example is the indexation of spending programs to macroeconomic variables, such as the price level or aggregate nominal income. In Latin America and the Caribbean, external constraints frequently occur in the form of minimum spending levels or budget shares for expenditure programs that are regarded as being of critical importance, such as health, education, or regional development. They commonly arise from past voter dissatisfaction and attempts to limit the government's discretionary decision-making power and to ensure its commitment to certain policies. Many of these constraints are enshrined in the constitution (see box 2.1 for the example of Costa Rica).

BOX 2.1

Constitutional mandates impose a high degree of rigidity in Costa Rica

During the past decade, Costa Rica has suffered from large and persistent fiscal deficits. In the aftermath of the 2008 global financial crisis, public spending increased and government revenues fell. The increase in public expenditures was a response to the crisis—a countercyclical fiscal stimulus like the ones followed by many Organisation for Economic Co-operation and Development and Latin American countries. However, the increase in public expenditure was driven by difficult-to-reverse rigid expenditure. Consequently, unlike other countries that managed to reduce their fiscal deficit when growth recovered, in Costa Rica the deficit remains very large, resulting in a steady increase in the public debt level and harming fiscal sustainability.

The inability to adjust when growth recovered was, in part, a consequence of the design of the stimulus package, as most expenditure measures implemented under the fiscal stimulus program were permanent. They included increases in public sector wages and pensions and new hires in the education, health, and security sectors. However, the inability to consolidate was also due to several legal and institutional mandates that created high rigidity in the budget.

In Costa Rica, the roots of budget rigidity can be traced back to the 1930s and 1940s, with the establishment of the first norms on social security and civil servant pensions. Over the past 70 years, multiple legal and administrative decisions have shaped the structure of today's budget. At least 10 relevant constitutional changes have impacted the budget and made it more rigid. All of them can be grouped around four topics related to financing:

- *Political parties:* There is currently an allocation of 0.19 percent of gross domestic product (GDP) (past GDP) to cover expenses of groups during presidential campaigns that receive a certain share of votes (5 percent).

- *Public education:* In 1997, the Congress approved the first amendment that increased public education financing to 6 percent of GDP. In 2011, that was raised to 8 percent of GDP. The public universities' financing model is also defined at the constitutional level, with reforms that started in the mid-1970s and continued during the 1980s. Although the constitution does not establish a specific level of funding for the Special Fund for Higher Education (FEES), in 2010 the negotiation between the government and the National Commission of Rectors resulted in a goal of 1.5 percent of GDP for the FEES once the Ministry of Education received the approved 8 percent of GDP. In other words, of the 8 percent allocated to education, 6.5 percent would remain in the hands of the Ministry of Education, while the remaining 1.5 percent would be assigned to public universities.

continued

Box 2.1, *continued*

- *Judicial branch:* A constitutional amendment in 1957 established that the minimum budgetary allocation to the judicial branch would be no less than 6 percent of current revenues. In recent years, however, the judicial power has been receiving somewhere between 9 percent and 10 percent of current revenues. Although this funding far exceeds the constitutional norm, authorities have frequently explained that since the 1970s, the judicial branch has been absorbing functions and responsibilities not originally envisaged in the 1957 reform. An example of this is the operation of the Judicial Investigation Agency under the budget of the court.

- *Local governments:* The most recent noneducation reform to the constitution established a transfer equivalent to 10 percent of current revenues from the central government to municipal regimes.

Source: Pacheco Jiménez 2019.

Such external constraints take the expenditures in question outside the scope of the political process that should determine the level and composition of government spending. In doing so, they enable policy makers to avoid tough choices (Weaver 1986). Also, they may be used as a political tool to tie the hands of future governments or legislatures that may have different preferences than the current leadership. However, they reduce the budgeting of the selected expenditures to mere forecasting exercises rather than deliberate political decisions. The practice creates rigidities because it makes it harder to change the parameters and the rules related to the expenditures.

These external constraints do have the advantage of increasing the predictability and reliability of government spending in areas that might otherwise be neglected or fall prey to rapid changes in political and macroeconomic conditions. Constraints may be necessary to encourage lower-level governments and private citizens to invest their own time and resources in such activities as education, health improvement, or local infrastructure. However, they should not become unchangeable for long periods of time. One solution would be to set a time frame for the external constraints, after which an expenditure review must be conducted to assess the continued need and adequacy of the relevant programs and constraints.

THE LEGAL VERSUS THE MANAGEMENT FUNCTIONS OF THE BUDGET

Every budget process embeds a tension between the legal and the management functions of the budget. The legal function emphasizes the need for government expenditures and revenues to be authorized by parliament and the conformity of all expenditures with formal rules and legal criteria. If the legal function is pursued to the extreme, budgeting becomes a perfectly legalistic but largely meaningless exercise of controlling government spending and revenues. As a management tool, the budget assigns resources to the various objectives of government policies and thus shows how the executive intends to meet its policy goals given the expected economic developments during a fiscal year. The management function of the budget calls for the possibility to react to new information and unforeseen developments during the fiscal year to ensure that these goals can be met effectively and efficiently.

A good balance between the two functions of the budget is necessary. One way to achieve this balance is to put less emphasis on the legality of each detailed expenditure item and more emphasis on the legality of the decision-making processes used to make choices between these items during the year, such as whether decisions are made by properly authorized actors and whether proper procedures are being followed. Line ministries or departments within them can be developed into budget management centers that manage their own budgets and authorize expenditures within certain limits during the fiscal year. The treasury would then oversee these centers rather than control each individual expenditure. In the line ministries, the staff of such management centers can include treasury representatives controlling the relevant decisions. This combination provides flexibility in the execution of the budget while ensuring conformity with the budget law.

Another aspect of the tension between the legal and the management functions can arise from entitlement and public sector wage benefit legislation, which has a large impact on rigidity. Entitlements define rights of individual citizens to receive resources from the government. They are created by substantive (nonfinancial) laws, but by resulting in financial obligations of the government, they have important consequences for the budget (Kraan 2004). If these rights are not properly defined or if they are interpreted as giving the beneficiaries a special status of being exempt from any necessary fiscal adjustment, they can result in downward budgetary rigidities enforced by the judicial system.

When entitlement legislation is poorly designed, the judicial system often gets involved, creating budgetary rigidities by interfering with budgetary management and control. For example, efforts by the national government of Costa Rica to adjust certain types of public expenditures downward during the country's fiscal crisis were repeatedly frustrated by rulings of the country's constitutional court declaring the adjustments unconstitutional. In 1997, the court defined a set of fundamental principles on acquired rights. An acquired right exists when "a thing—material or immaterial—whether it is a previously alien property or a right that was previously nonexistent has entered the patrimonial sphere of the person, so that the latter experiences a verifiable advantage or benefit" (Pacheco Jiménez 2019, 32). In other words, if a worker already receives an incentive, all that was received in the past cannot be affected by any type of measure. Similarly, Echeverry (2019) reports that the 1991 constitution of Colombia created a mechanism by which judges at all levels of the justice system can issue mandates on the national budget benefiting individual citizens. However, the Colombia case study for this report also shows that rigidities can be reduced over time, when there is political will to free policy makers from the straightjacket of entitlements to face crisis situations that require discretionary policy.

Transfers of tax revenues from the central government to regional and local governments that are predetermined by legal rules are a source of rigidity, but they can provide necessary protection to lower-level governments. Taking the revenues out of the scope of the annual budget process and the political process is useful and desirable because it strengthens the reliability and predictability of revenue flows from the central government to the level of regional and local governments. Leaving such transfers to the discretion of the central government may seem convenient and may appear to give the central government more flexibility and discretionary power. However, it exposes lower-level governments to macroeconomic risks, which they cannot bear efficiently. Because lower-level governments have significantly less borrowing power, their capacity to deal with major shocks is much weaker than that of the central government (Foremny and von Hagen 2013).

The predetermined transfers from the central government to local governments also protect the central government from opportunistic behavior at the regional and local levels. In the absence of fixed rules, regional and local governments may overspend their allocations quickly and then demand bailouts from the central government, threatening to end public services in critical areas such as health or education. Given the high social and political cost of shutting down such services, the central government will find it hard to resist such demands. In the end, the central government may have a greater ability to manage its budget with fixed rules of revenue sharing in place.

NOTE

1. Using real per capita GDP as a proxy for the country's income and the real per capita public wage bill as a proxy for the average wage in the public sector, we observe a positive association between the two variables over time.

REFERENCES

Balassa, Bela. 1964. "The Purchasing Power Parity Doctrine: A Reappraisal." *Journal of Political Economy* 72 (6): 584–96.

Bhagwati, Jagdish. 1984. "Why Are Services Cheaper in the Poor Countries?" *Economic Journal* 94 (374): 279–86.

Cetrángolo, Oscar, Juan Pablo Jiménez, and Ramiro Ruiz del Castillo. 2010. "Rigidities and Fiscal Space in Latin America: A Comparative Case Study." Series Macroeconomía del Desarrollo 97, Economic Commission for Latin America and the Caribbean (ECLAC), Santiago, Chile.

Echeverry, Juan Carlos. 2019. "Combating Budget Inflexibility in Colombia 2000–2016." Background Report for Regional Study on Budget Rigidities in Latin America, unpublished paper, World Bank, Washington, DC.

Echeverry, Juan Carlos, L. Fergusson, and P. Querubín. 2005. "Budget Inflexibility." Documento CEDE 2005-52, Universidad de los Andes, Bogotá, Colombia.

Echeverry, Juan Carlos, Jorge Alexander Bonilla, and Andres Moya. 2006. "Rigideces institucionales y flexibilidad presupuestaria: los casos de Argentina, Colombia, México y Perú." Documento CEDE 2006-33, Universidad de los Andes, Bogotá, Colombia.

Foremny, Dirk, and Jurgen von Hagen. 2013. "Sub-national Budgetary Discipline During Times of Crisis: The Impact of Fiscal Rules and Tax Autonomy." In *Fiscal Relations Across Government Levels in Times of Crisis—Making Compatible Fiscal Decentralization and Budgetary Discipline*. Economic Papers 501, European Economy. Brussels: European Commission. https://ec.europa.eu/economy_finance/publications/economic_paper/2013/pdf/ecp501_en.pdf.

Garrett, Thomas, and Russell Rhine. 2006. "On the Size and Growth of Government." *Federal Reserve Bank of St. Louis Review,* 88 (1).

Herrera, S., and J. Velasco. 2019. "Budget Rigidity in LAC: A Proposed New Measure for Empirical Analysis." Background Report for Regional Study on Budget Rigidities in Latin America, unpublished paper, World Bank, Washington, DC.

International Monetary Fund. 2019. World Economic Outlook database. https://www.imf.org /en/Publications/SPROLLs/world-economic-outlook-databases#sort=%40imfdate%20 descending

Kraan, Dirk-Jan. 2004. "Off-Budget and Tax Expenditures." *OECD Journal on Budgeting* 4 (1): 121–42.

Pacheco Jiménez, J. F. 2019. "Budget Rigidities: Case Study of Costa Rica." Unpublished paper.

Rodrik, Dani. 2000. "What Drives Public Employment in Developing Countries?" *Review of Development Economics* 4 (3): 229–43.

Samuelson, P. 1964. "Theoretical Notes on Trade Problems." *Review of Economics and Statistics* 46 (2): 145–54.

von Hagen, Jürgen, and Yao Chen. 2019. "Budget Rigidities and Fiscal Performance in Latin America and the Caribbean." Background Report for Regional Study on Budget Rigidities in Latin America, unpublished paper, World Bank, Washington, DC.

Weaver, R. Kent. 1986. "The Politics of Blame Avoidance." *Journal of Public Policy* 6 (4): 371–98.

3 Measurement of Rigidity and Stylized Facts

The existing literature on spending rigidity aggregates the different components of actual expenditure—such as compensation of employees, social security benefits, transfers to subnational governments, and debt service—to calculate the rigid part of the expenditure (Echeverry, Bonilla, and Moya 2006; Cetrángolo and Jiménez 2009; Vegh et al. 2017). This approach assumes that the totality of these expenditures is beyond the policy maker's control, which may be plausible in the case of interest payments, but may be less applicable in the case of public wages, social security benefits, and other expenditures. The traditional approach of aggregating wages, pensions, and interest payments shows that expenditure rigidity, as a percentage of total spending, remained stable from 2000 to 2017 (figure 3.1).[1]

When examining the different components—namely, wages, pensions, and interest payments—there is significant heterogeneity across regions. In wages, East Asia and Pacific (EAP) and Europe and Central Asia (ECA) show a declining trend; Latin America and the Caribbean (LAC) and Sub-Saharan Africa (SSA) show remarkable stability, although at different levels; and the Middle East and North Africa (MENA) and South Asia show some variability (figure 3.2). Pensions show a clear rising trend, especially in ECA and LAC (figure 3.3). Interest payments show a declining trend until 2010, and an increase in 2017, with the rise of world interest rates and rising debt levels (figure 3.4).

This report proposes a new measure of rigidity based on the notion that public spending can be separated into two parts: (a) a structural component that is determined by long-run economic fundamentals and (b) a nonstructural component that is determined by policy decisions or short-run effects of variables associated with the business cycle. The structural determinants of the wage bill may differ from those of other components of spending, such as pension payments or transfers to subnational governments, or affect them with a different sign. For instance, although the wage bill will be positively related to a demographic variable that captures the size of the working-age population, pension payments will be negatively associated with it. Alternatively, the wage bill may not be related to private sector participation in the pension payment system, but public pension

FIGURE 3.1
Rigid expenditure across regions, 2000–17

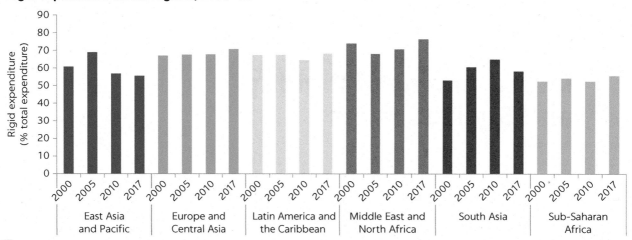

Source: Herrera and Velasco 2019.

FIGURE 3.2
Wage bills across regions, 2000–17

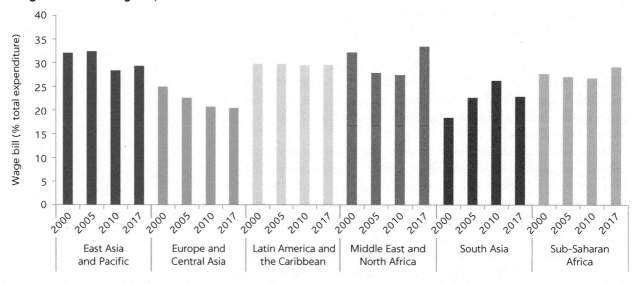

Source: Herrera and Velasco 2019.

payments will be related. The structural component is determined by long-run economic fundamentals beyond the policy maker's control and will be interpreted as the rigid level of spending.[2] The nonstructural component is the difference between the observed and the structural, and is determined by short-run transitory factors related to the business or political cycles. The degree of rigidity of spending will be approximated by the ratio of structural spending to total spending. The nonstructural component of wages or pension payments provides an indication of the discretion that policy makers have used in the past, causing deviations of total spending from the structural level.

FIGURE 3.3

Pension payments across regions, 2000–17

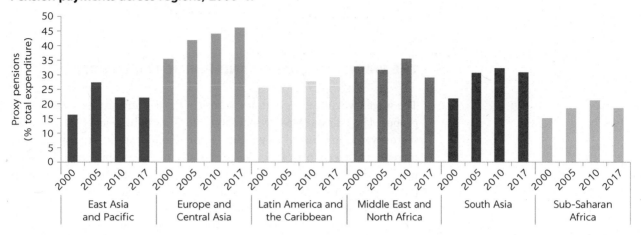

Source: Herrera and Velasco 2019.

FIGURE 3.4

Interest payments across regions, 2000–17

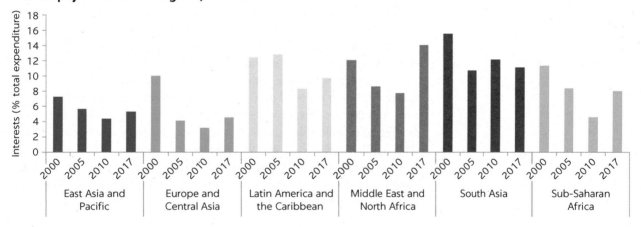

Source: Herrera and Velasco 2019.

In the following sections, the structural components of each of the major categories are estimated, their evolution over time is shown, and cross-country comparisons are presented. The structural components of each category are then aggregated, with interest payments, to build a comprehensive measure of rigidity. The same methodology (described in the appendix) is used throughout the discussion, consisting of estimating econometric models for the determinants of the spending aggregate and taking the predicted level for each country as the structural component.[3] To avoid having negative values for the nonstructural component, which is the residual, the estimated equations are shifted in a fashion like corrected ordinary least squares;[4] this implies that spending levels are adjusted, taking as reference levels those of the more efficient countries or those with lower spending levels. Stylized facts regarding the relationship between country rigidity and fiscal outcomes are also presented, while the relationship between budget rigidity and stabilization and medium-term sustainability is discussed in the last section.

THE WAGE BILL: WAGES AND PUBLIC EMPLOYMENT

The wage level increases with the wealth of the country, in line with theories proposed by Balassa (1964), Samuelson (1964), and Bhagwati (1984). If public sector wages are linked to private sector remuneration, they should also increase with a country's income level. Using real per capita gross domestic product (GDP) as a proxy for the country's income and the real per capita public wage bill as a proxy for the average wage in the public sector, a positive association between the two variables is observed, as shown in the previous chapter (see figure 2.2). On the basis of these theories, and following previous literature (Shelton 2007), Herrera and Velasco (2019) estimate a structural model of the determinants of public wages, using as explanatory variables GDP per capita and country characteristics such as the population, population density, demographic composition (youth and elderly), and the degree of openness of the economy.[5]

The predicted wage is interpreted as the expected structural component of the public wage for each country, given its income level and other country characteristics. It provides an estimation of the government wage level given the structure of the economy and population. This level is determined by structural factors that are not under direct government control, and hence create rigidity in the level of spending. The difference between the observed level and the structural component is the nonstructural component, which is affected by policy decisions—that is, it is under the government's control. The rigidity in this case would not come from economic factors but from political economy considerations. The lower the share of the structural component, the more flexibility policy makers will have to make adjustments if they have the political will to do so.

FIGURE 3.5

Structural component of the public wage bill as a percentage of the actual wage bill, by region, 2000–17

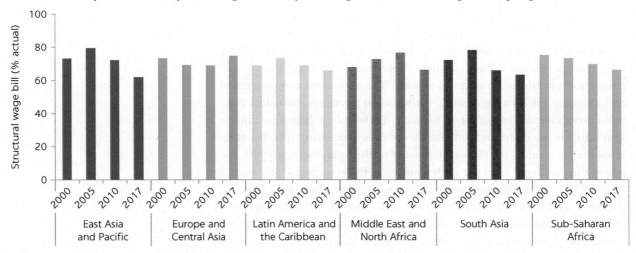

Source: Herrera and Velasco 2019.

In general, across different regions, the structural component of the wage bill decreases as a driver of total spending after 2005, probably because of the countercyclical policies adopted during the Great Recession period (figure 3.5). In Europe and Central Asia, the share of the structural component of wages increases again in 2017, reflecting the fiscal adjustment undertaken in the region that limited spending. Within Latin America and the Caribbean, there is great heterogeneity in the share of the structural component of wages within total wages: it varies from less than 50 percent in Haiti to about 90 percent in Panama (figure 3.6). Within the spectrum of countries, several small countries in Latin America and the Caribbean are at the higher end, with more rigid spending. However, countries with nonstructural factors dominating the wage bill (for example, Argentina, The Bahamas, Ecuador, and Haiti—all with ratios under 60 percent), suggest a higher relative importance of nonstructural determinants of the wage bill in these cases.

Changes in the share of the structural component in wages from 2000 to 2017 indicate heterogeneity in the management of government wages. In some countries, the structural fundamentals are more decisive in the evolution of wages, while in other countries they appear to demonstrate the opposite (figure 3.6). Based on the evolution of wages, there are three country groupings: (a) countries in which the wage converges to the structural level; (b) countries in which the wage diverges from the structural level; and (c) countries in which divergence follows a period of convergence to the structural level.

In the first of the three country groupings—composed of Antigua and Barbuda, Brazil, Colombia, Mexico, Panama, and Suriname—differentiated on the basis of the evolution of wages, it is worth noting that, despite having converging trends, countries may have different rigidity levels. For instance, Brazil and Mexico have a lower wage rigidity, about 70 percent, while in Colombia and Panama, between 80 percent and 90 percent of the wage is explained by structural factors.

FIGURE 3.6

Structural component of the public wage bill as a percentage of the actual wage bill in LAC, 2000–17

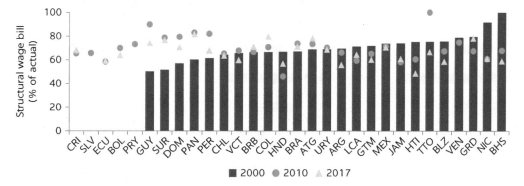

Source: Herrera and Velasco 2019.
Note: CHL = Chile; COL = Colombia; CRI = Costa Rica; DOM = Dominican Republic; ECU = Ecuador; GRD = Grenada; GTM = Guatemala; GUY = Guyana; HND = Honduras; HTI = Haiti; JAM = Jamaica; LCA = St. Lucia; MEX = Mexico; NIC = Nicaragua; PAN = Panama; PER = Peru; PRY = Paraguay; SLV = El Salvador; SUR = Suriname; TTO = Trinidad and Tobago; URY = Uruguay; VCT = St. Vincent and the Grenadines; VEN = Venezuela, RB.

The second group of countries, composed mostly of Central American countries plus the Andean nations (such as Bolivia, Ecuador, and República Bolivariana de Venezuela), is characterized by a clear decreasing trend of the structural component. This group shows a generalized reduction, from about 80 percent to 60 percent, with the lowest level in Honduras, at about 50 percent.

The third group of countries is characterized by converging and then diverging trends at the structural level. Argentina and Chile initially show a stable or converging level, until 2005; then there is a clear trend for wages to deviate from the structural component, coinciding with the boom in commodity prices. Peru shows a convergence throughout the boom, but then diverges after 2014 with the commodity price bust.

PUBLIC EMPLOYMENT

So far, it has been assumed that wage bill rigidity emanates from the wage level, but rigidity can also originate from the level of employment. This analysis helps separate the changes in the wage bill between quantity (employment) and price (wages). Work contracts make labor adjustments difficult and costly. Public employment, measured as the percentage of the labor force that is employed by the public sector, shows different levels across regions (figure 3.7) and over time. The literature that examines the determinants of public employment is based on the work of Dani Rodrik, who models public employment as a policy tool to provide insurance against exposure to external, undiversifiable risk (Rodrik 2000) or as a tool to redistribute rents or compensate for inequality or social fragmentation (Alesina, Baqir, and Easterly 2000).

FIGURE 3.7

Public employment as a percentage of the labor force, by region

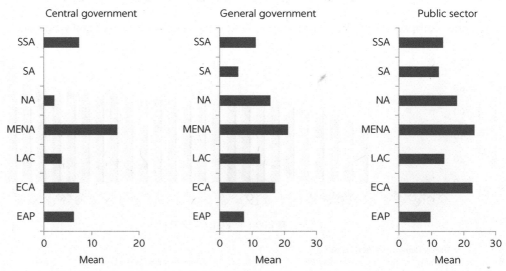

Source: Herrera and Munoz 2019a.
Note: EAP = East Asia and Pacific; ECA = Europe and Central Asia; LAC = Latin American and the Caribbean; MENA = Middle East and North Africa; NA = North America; SA = South Asia; SSA = Sub-Saharan Africa.

The empirical analysis of the determinants of public employment done for this report (Herrera and Munoz 2019a) shows that public employment is negatively associated with country size by population and positively associated with income level.[6] Verifying Rodrik's hypothesis that public employment may be used as a tool to mitigate a country's exposure to undiversifiable external risk,[7] it is determined that the country's openness to trade is heterogeneously related to public employment: it is positively associated with public employment in low- and middle-income countries, but inversely related in high-income countries. In the case of ethnic fractionalization, a negative association is found, implying that more fragmented countries have lower public sector employment, while the age-dependency ratio and income inequality are not statistically significant correlates of public employment.[8]

Levels of public employment can be predicted for each country, given its income, population, and openness to trade, and compared with the observed levels to see if there is "excess public employment." In general, public employment in Latin American countries is below the predicted levels. In the Middle East and North Africa, public employment is above the predicted levels, particularly in the Arab Republic of Egypt and the Islamic Republic of Iran. Public employment in the East Asia and Pacific economies is significantly below the predicted levels, particularly in Hong Kong SAR, China; Japan; the Republic of Korea; and Mongolia. The countries of Europe and Central Asia also show higher-than-predicted public employment: mostly Latvia, Norway, Romania, Sweden, and Ukraine. In Sub-Saharan Africa, public employment appears below predicted levels, with the notable exceptions of Botswana and South Africa. But in Latin America and the Caribbean, Suriname, Argentina, República Bolivariana de Venezuela, and Trinidad and Tobago (figure 3.8) show significant deviations above predicted levels. The deviations from predicted levels are positively correlated with the union density rate (figure 3.9),[9] implying that some of the factors behind these deviations are political and institutional in nature.

FIGURE 3.8

Deviation of observed public employment from predicted levels, based on fundamentals in LAC

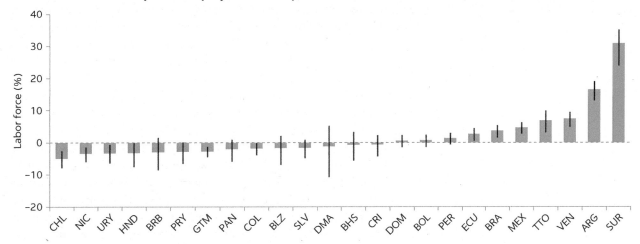

Source: Herrera and Munoz 2019a.
Note: Line indicates a 95 percent confidence interval. ARG = Argentina; BHS = The Bahamas; BLZ = Belize; BOL = Bolivia; BRA = Brazil; BRB = Barbados; CHI = Chile; COL = Colombia; CRI = Costa Rica; DMA = Dominica; DOM = Dominican Republic; ECU = Ecuador; GTM = Guatemala; HND = Honduras; LAC = Latin America and the Caribbean; MEX = Mexico; NIC = Nicaragua; PAN = Panama; PER = Peru; PRY = Paraguay; SLV = El Salvador; SUR = Suriname; TTO = Trinidad and Tobago; URY = Uruguay; VEN = Venezuela, RB.

FIGURE 3.9

Union density and public employment

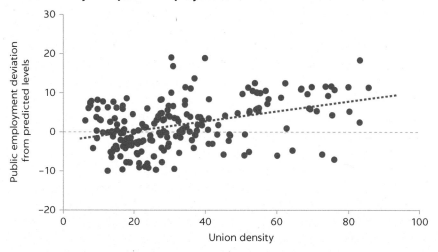

Source: Herrera and Munoz 2019a.

Public employment is not a major distortion in most countries in Latin America and the Caribbean, except in Argentina, Suriname, Trinidad and Tobago, and República Bolivariana de Venezuela. Most of the wage bill excess or rigidity is derived from public wage levels. Cerda and Pessino (2018) and Izquierdo, Pessino, and Vuletin (2018) show that the wage premium in Latin America on average is 34 percent, while Gindling et al. (2019) report a regional average of 26 percent. Despite the significant differences due to different samples and methodologies, these levels are extremely high when compared with world averages of about 10 percent (IMF 2016).

PENSION PAYMENTS

This section discusses the estimation of the structural component of government pension payments and compares it with observed levels, to gauge the space for policy action in this category of spending. Pension payments, like wages, show a positive association with GDP per capita across the world (figure 3.10), as they are derived from higher wages and different demographic compositions as societies become wealthier. The structural level was estimated using a fixed-effect model that includes demographic factors, the wage level of the economy, and the type of retirement system that prevails in the country (that is, whether it is public or private, or a pay-as-you-go versus individual savings).[10]

The structural component of pension payments is calculated with the model predictions, and it is noted that the ratio of this component to the observed payments in Latin America and the Caribbean is 74 percent; the remaining 26 percent is the regional aggregate of flexibility for pension adjustment. The ratio of the structural component to total pension payments indicates the relative importance of economic fundamentals in driving actual pension payments. Across regions, there is no discernible pattern from 2000 to 2017 (figure 3.11). Although Europe and Central Asia and the Middle East and North Africa show a declining trend in the structural component,

FIGURE 3.10

Public pension payments per capita and GDP per capita

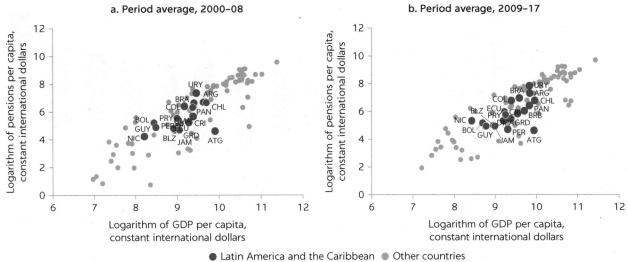

a. Period average, 2000–08

b. Period average, 2009–17

● Latin America and the Caribbean ● Other countries

Source: Herrera and Velasco 2019.
Note: ARG = Argentina; ATG = Antigua and Barbuda; BLZ = Belize; BOL = Bolivia; BRA = Brazil; BRB = Barbados; CHL = Chile; COL = Colombia; CRI = Costa Rica; DMA = Dominica; ECU = Ecuador; GRD = Grenada; GUY = Guyana; JAM = Jamaica; NIC = Nicaragua; PAN = Panama; PER = Peru; PRY = Paraguay; URY = Uruguay.

FIGURE 3.11

Structural component as a percentage of public pension payments by region, 2000–17

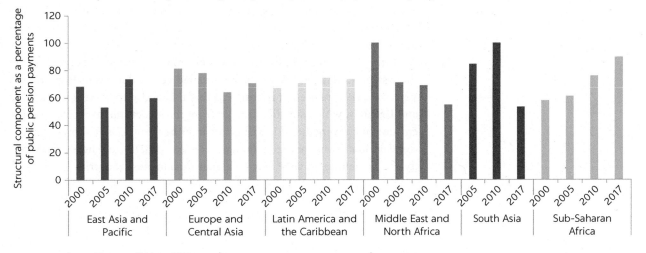

Source: Herrera and Velasco 2019.

Sub-Saharan Africa shows a rising trend and Latin America and the Caribbean shows remarkable stability.

Within Latin America and the Caribbean, there is significant heterogeneity. In 2017, the ratio was close to 100 percent in Chile, Panama, and Peru, implying that pension payments were almost exclusively driven by structural factors, while the ratio was between 40 percent and 50 percent in Ecuador and Nicaragua and the ratio oscillated around 65 percent in Argentina, Brazil, and Uruguay.

FIGURE 3.12

Structural component of pensions in LAC, 2000–17

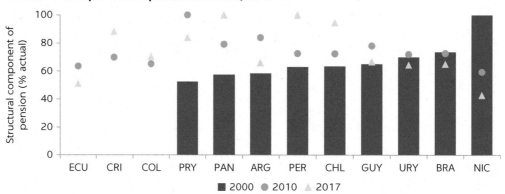

Source: Herrera and Velasco 2019.
Note: ARG = Argentina; BRA = Brazil; CHL = Chile; COL = Colombia; CRI = Costa Rica; ECU = Ecuador; GUY = Guyana; LAC = Latin America and the Caribbean; NIC = Nicaragua; PAN = Panama; PER = Peru; PRY = Paraguay; URY = Uruguay.

The relative importance of structural factors changes over time in each country (figure 3.12), although the trends are less volatile than in the case of wages. This report focuses on two groups of countries. The first group, in which structural factors gain importance as drivers of pension expenditure and the ratio of structural spending to actual levels reaches 100 percent over time, includes Chile, Panama, and Peru. Although Chile and Panama show a gradual increase to the structural level, in Peru convergence was achieved in less time. The second group includes countries in which the structural components decrease in importance as drivers of pensions, and hence the ratio diverges from the structural level. This is the case for Argentina, Ecuador, and Nicaragua, which show a sustained divergence from their structural levels. When more detailed yearly data from Herrera and Velasco (2019) are used, it is observed that this is also the case for Colombia and Uruguay, which steadily diverge from the structural level after a short episode of convergence.[11] Brazil is not in either group, as it shows a mixed trend oscillating in the region (as a percentage of GDP), and hence the rigidity as a percentage of GDP may be higher than in most countries.

TRANSFERS TO SUBNATIONAL GOVERNMENTS

Transfers to subnational governments (SNGs) constitute another category of spending that is inflexible and generally arises from constitutional mandates. For this report, namely, the aggregation of rigid spending in the budget for cross-country and intertemporal comparisons, this aggregate presents empirical difficulties because most of the transfers—which are for paying teachers, doctors, and nurses—are included in the wage aggregate reported already. Hence, the structural component of the central government's transfers to SNGs is not included in the aggregate measure of expenditure rigidity to avoid double-counting, but they are discussed in the report because decentralization is a critical source of central government expenditure rigidity in some countries in the region (Brazil, Colombia, and Mexico).

The structural component of transfers to SNGs was estimated, following existing literature on determinants of this category of spending (Eyraud and

Lusinyan 2013) and using as explanatory variables: (a) the GDP per capita to capture the Balassa-Samuelson wage effect; (b) the vertical fiscal gap, defined as the difference between the percentage of the spending undertaken by the SNG and the percentage of the revenue raised by the SNG, as a percentage of total SNG spending;[12] (c) the capacity of SNGs to raise their own revenues, which captures the effect of expanding the scale or the envelope of operations of the SNGs; and (d) political economy variables that capture the relative power of local governments vis-à-vis the central government and a measure of inequality in the distribution of resources.

Results show (see table A.4 in the appendix) that higher GDP per capita is associated with higher transfers to SNGs, as happens with other public spending components. Because transfers are made to pay for services that are labor intensive, higher wages in richer countries might explain this positive association. A larger vertical gap is associated with higher transfers because the imbalance between expenditure responsibility and capacity to generate revenue implies more transfers from the central government. The positive association between SNGs' own revenues and transfers from the central government can be interpreted as a "crowding-in" effect. The more relative power of regional or local governments vis-à-vis the central one is associated with higher transfers.[13] Although inequality in the distribution of resources is not significant, its interaction with the division of power is, meaning that inequality is significant when there is more decentralization of political power.

The data availability only allows estimating the structural transfers to SNGs in a few countries. According to these estimations, structural central government transfers to SNGs in Latin America and the Caribbean range from 58 percent of actual transfers in Chile to 83 percent in Costa Rica (figure 3.13). These results suggest that central governments in the region transfer to SNGs significantly more than the amounts indicated by the structural factors, both in highly decentralized countries (Brazil, Colombia, or Peru) and in centralized ones (Chile).

FIGURE 3.13

Structural central government transfers to subnational governments

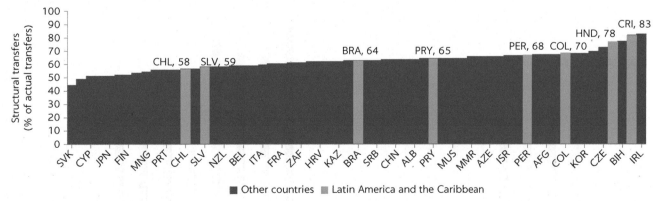

Source: Herrera and Velasco 2019.
Note: Average of available figures between 2010 and 2016; AFG = Afghanistan; ALB = Albania; AZE = Azerbaijan; BEL = Belgium; BIH = Bosnia and Herzegovina; BRA = Brazil; CHL = Chile; CHN = China; COL = Colombia; CYP = Cyprus; CZE = Czech Republic; FIN = Finland; FRA = France; HRV = Croatia; IRL = Ireland; ITA = Italy; JPN = Japan; KAZ = Kazakhstan; KOR = Republic of Korea; ISR = Israel; MMR = Myanmar; MNG = Mongolia; MUS = Mauritius; NZL = New Zealand; PER = Peru; PRT = Portugal; PRY = Paraguay; SLV = El Salvador; SRB = Serbia; SVK = Slovak Republic; ZAF = South Africa.

AGGREGATE MEASURE OF RIGIDITY

A more complete picture of total rigidity in the budget can be obtained by aggregating pensions, wages, and interest payments. Of note are the following three major points:

- In general, countries in Latin America and the Caribbean do not have a significantly higher share of rigid expenditure than other regions when measured as a percentage of spending (figure 3.1 shows rigid spending as traditionally measured, and figure 3.14 shows rigid spending measured with the structural approximation proposed in this report), but the rigidity is lower when scaled by GDP (figure 3.15).

FIGURE 3.14

Total structural public spending as a percentage of expenditure across regions, 2000–17

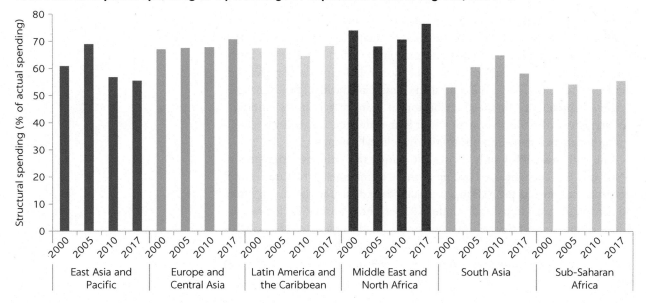

Source: Estimates from Herrera and Velasco 2019.

FIGURE 3.15

Total rigid public spending as a percentage of GDP across regions, 2000–17

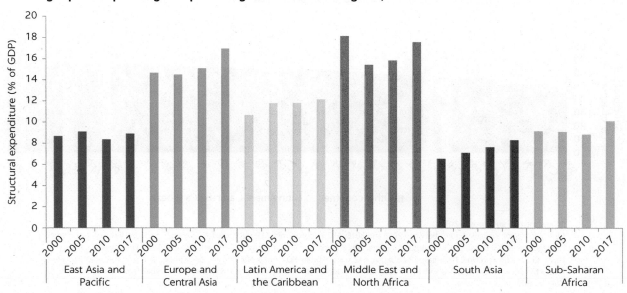

Source: Herrera and Velasco 2019.

- Within Latin America and the Caribbean, there is enormous heterogeneity, with the share of rigid spending fluctuating between 5 percent of GDP in Haiti to almost 18 percent in Argentina, Bolivia, and Brazil (figure 3.16). As a percentage of total spending, the range is even higher, from 23 percent in Haiti to 70 percent in Costa Rica and Guatemala (figure 3.17). Expenditures in Haiti are dominated by nonstructural factors, while Argentina, Bolivia, and Brazil show the largest shares of structural components of spending.
- The space of expenditure adjustment is significantly higher than implied by previous rigidity estimates, when the entire aggregate of wages and pensions is included (table 3.1). From previous levels of rigidity of 90 percent or more, the results show levels of around 50 percent in countries such as Brazil and Colombia.

FIGURE 3.16

Total rigid public spending in LAC, 2000–17

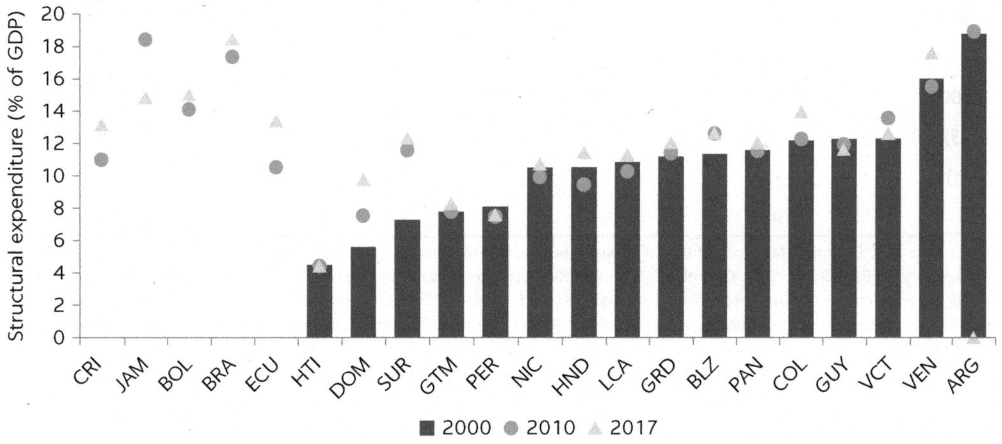

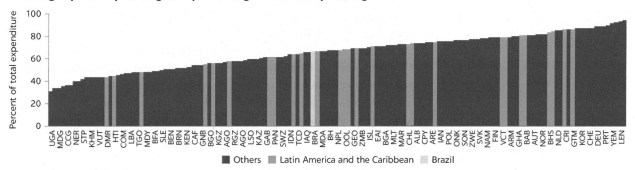

Source: Herrera and Velasco 2019.

Note: ARG = Argentina; BLZ = Belize; BOL = Bolivia; BRA = Brazil; COL = Colombia; CRI = Costa Rica; DOM = Dominican Republic; ECU = Ecuador; GRD = Grenada; GTM = Guatemala; GUY = Guyana; HND = Honduras; HTI = Haiti; JAM = Jamaica; LCA = St. Lucia; NIC = Nicaragua; PAN = Panama; PER = Peru; SUR = Suriname; VCT = St. Vincent and the Grenadines; VEN = Venezuela, RB.

FIGURE 3.17

Total rigid public spending as a percentage of actual spending

Source: Herrera and Velasco 2019.

Note: Rigid spending is wages+interest+other current expenditure. AGO = Angola; ALB = Albania; ARE = United Arab Emirates; ARM = Armenia; AUT = Austria; BEN = Benin; BFA = Burkina Faso; BGD = Bangladesh; BGR = Bulgaria; BHS = The Bahamas; BIH = Bosnia and Herzegovina; BRA = Brazil; BRB = Barbados; BRN = Brunei Darussalam; CAF = Central African Republic; CHE = Switzerland; CHL = Chile; COG= the Republic of Congo; COL = Colombia; COM = Comoros; CPV = Cabo Verde; CRI = Costa Rica; DEU = Germany; DMA = Dominica; DNK = Denmark; ERI = Eritrea; FIN = Finland; GAB = Gabon; GEO = Georgia; GHA = Ghana; GMB = The Gambia; GNB = Guinea-Bissau; GTM = Guatemala; HTI = Haiti; IDN = Indonesia; IRN = Islamic Republic of Iran; IRQ = Iraq; ISL = Iceland; KAZ = Kazakhstan; KEN = Kenya; KGZ = Kyrgyz Republic; KHM = Cambodia; KOR = Republic of Korea; LBN = Lebanon; LBR = Liberia; LSO = Lesotho; MAR = Morocco; MDA = Moldova; MDG = Madagascar; MDV = Maldives; MLT = Malta; MOZ = Mozambique; NAM = Namibia; NER = Niger; NLD = Netherlands; NOR = Norway; NPL = Nepal; PAN = Panama; POL = Poland; PRT = Portugal; SDN = Sudan; SLE = Sierra Leone; STP = São Tomé and Príncipe; SVK = Slovak Republic; SWZ = Swaziland; TCD = Chad; TGO = Togo; UGA = Uganda; VCT = St. Vincent and the Grenadines; VUT = Vanuatu; YEM = Republic of Yemen; ZMB = Zambia; ZWE = Zimbabwe.

TABLE 3.1 **Spending rigidity in LAC as reported in previous literature**

COUNTRY	PERCENT OF PRIMARY SPENDING	PERCENT OF GDP	STRUCTURAL RIGIDITY AS PERCENT OF PRIMARY SPENDING	STRUCTURAL RIGIDITY AS PERCENT OF GDP
Argentina (2003)	80	24	61	14
Brazil (2015)	94	20	50	19
Brazil (2003)	87	n.a.	51	21
Bolivia (2006)	75	23	49	15
Chile (2003)	66	14	45	10
Chile (2014)	65	n.a.	46	11
Colombia (2006)	91	22	45	13
Colombia (2000)	80	13	46	12
Colombia (1990)	68	6	n.a.	n.a.
Costa Rica (2006)	95	11	79	12
Ecuador (2006)	80	27	54	12
Guatemala (2006)	64	8	n.a.	n.a.
Honduras (2006)	76	14	n.a.	n.a.
Mexico (2003)	76	18	n.a.	n.a.
Mexico (2014)	72	18	n.a.	n.a.
Peru (2006)	91	13	41	8

Sources: For 2003 Argentina, Colombia, Mexico, and Peru (Echeverry, Bonilla, and Moya 2006). For Brazil and Chile: World Bank Public Expenditure Reviews (World Bank 2016; 2017). Colombia 1990 and 2000 data from Lozano (2000). Bolivia, Costa Rica, Ecuador, Guatemala, and Honduras (Cetrángolo and Jiménez 2009). Compilation of papers by Almeida (2009a, 2009b) on Bolivia and Ecuador; by Echeverry, Bonilla, and Moya (2006) on Peru and Colombia; and by Cabrera and Fuentes (2009) on Costa Rica, Guatemala, and Honduras. Data for structural rigidity are from Herrera and Velasco (2019).
Note: GDP = gross domestic product; LAC = Latin America and the Caribbean; n.a. = not applicable.

Using a proxy for pension payments enables the expansion of the number of countries in Latin America and the Caribbean in the sample (figures 3.16 and 3.17).[14] In doing so, it was found that several Caribbean countries—such as The Bahamas, Belize, St. Vincent and the Grenadines, and Trinidad and Tobago—have the lowest ratio (below 40 percent) of the structural component within total spending. Argentina and Brazil are not much higher. However, Guatemala, Panama, and Peru are at the high end of the spectrum.

The structural component of spending, when measured as a share of total spending and of GDP, shows that variability is lower across countries in Latin America and the Caribbean than other regions (figures 3.14 and 3.15). A country such as Guatemala can have a high rigid share of spending that becomes lower when shown as a percentage of GDP, given that total spending is lower as a share of GDP than in the rest of the region. On the contrary, Argentina and Trinidad and Tobago, which have moderate levels of structural spending components, see their rigidity level magnified by the size of spending in GDP.

Budget rigidities lead to higher levels of government spending, which may be associated with higher taxes, higher debt, or both (Cetrángolo, Jiménez, and del Castillo 2010; Echeverry, Bonilla, and Moya 2006; Mattina and Gunnarsson 2007). Figure 3.18 shows that for the large sample of countries and over time, higher rigidity is associated with higher spending. Because higher spending needs to be financed, it is also associated with higher tax rates (figure 3.19). Higher rigidity is also associated with higher deficits

FIGURE 3.18

Government spending and rigid expenditure as a percentage of total expenditure

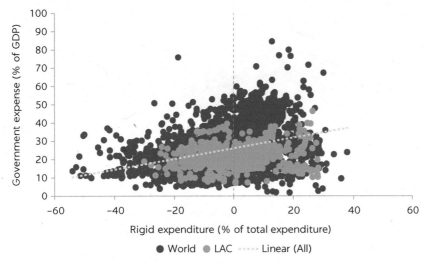

Source: Herrera and Munoz 2019b.
Note: Y = 26.10 (0.21) + 0.29 (0.01) X, standard error in parentheses. LAC = Latin America and the Caribbean.

FIGURE 3.19

Value added tax rates and rigid expenditure

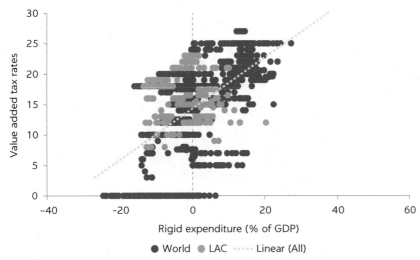

Source: Herrera and Munoz 2019b.
Note: Y = 14.29 (0.17) + 0.42 (0.02) X, standard error in parentheses. LAC = Latin America and the Caribbean.

(figure 3.20) and higher debt (figure 3.21). These correlations imply a vicious circle of rigidity to higher spending and debt, which implies higher debt service, which implies more rigidity.

Several authors argue that budget rigidities introduce inefficiencies (Echeverry, Bonilla, and Moya 2006; Mattina and Gunnarsson 2007). Figure 3.22 shows a clear negative association between rigidity and the efficiency of the public sector: countries with more rigid spending have lower

FIGURE 3.20

Fiscal balance and rigid expenditure

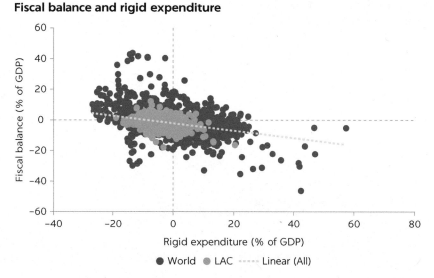

Source: Herrera and Munoz 2019b.
Note: Y = −2.06 (0.10) + −0.24 (0.02) X, standard error in parentheses. LAC = Latin America and the Caribbean.

FIGURE 3.21

General government gross debt and rigid expenditure

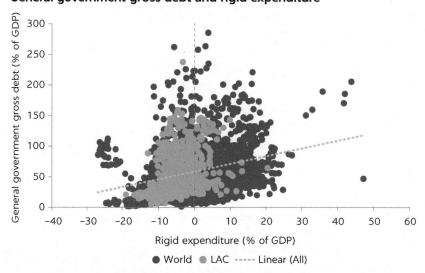

Source: Herrera and Munoz 2019b.
Note: Y = 57.48 (0.66) + 1.26 (0.08) X, standard error in parentheses. GDP = gross domestic product; LAC = Latin America and the Caribbean.

efficiency scores. Efficiency is measured by technical efficiency, defined as the distance between observed education, health, or infrastructure output levels and the production efficiency frontier—that is, the maximum output level attainable with a given level of input.[15] It might be worthwhile to note that inefficiency can also lead to budget rigidities. For instance, inefficient public teachers or doctors may become constituents for minimum spending rules on education and health.

FIGURE 3.22

Public sector efficiency and rigid expenditure

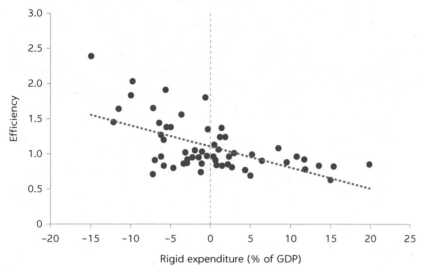

Source: Herrera and Munoz 2019b.
Note: Y = 1.11 (0.04) − 0.03 (0.01) X, standard error in parentheses.

NOTES

1. For simplicity and to be able to compare measures across a large set of countries, we initially employ a minimal and generally accepted measure of rigidities (Vegh et al. 2017): the sum of public wages, social benefits, and debt services as a share of GDP. Measuring budget rigidity is difficult because of the legal and political dimensions involved and the need to judge their relative strength, which varies across countries and over time. Ideally, we would like to have a measure that proxies the constraints imposed by legislation and the political feasibility of changing it. To do this, we would use a wide definition of budget rigidities—one that encompasses all institutional, political, and legal constraints. But this would be extremely difficult to identify and quantify in a way that would be comparable across countries. Differences in national institutional settings represent a major obstacle to systematically collecting international data for comparison purposes, as comparing budget rigidity across countries requires making judgments about the strength of similar constraints in different institutional settings and political realities.

2. The estimation of the long-run or structural relationships is based on panel data for up to 166 countries during the period 1980–2017. Data availability varies for each type of spending, so it considers both individual country and cross-country relationships between the variables.

3. The explanatory variables are those described in the previous section, but they are constrained by data availability. Although the proxies for level of development—such as GDP per capita, population, or demographic composition—are widely available, others such as the opacity of the budget process or delays in the budget negotiation process, which originate budget rigidity, are difficult to approximate.

4. Corrected ordinary least squares are typically used to estimate deterministic frontiers in cross-sectional data. This procedure is explained by Greene: http://pages.stern.nyu.edu/~wgreene/FrontierModeling/SurveyPapers/Greene-FRONTIERS.pdf.

5. The estimated model is presented in the appendix. The model was also tested for possible asymmetry in the response of wages to GDP per capita, depending on whether GDP was going up or down, or whether GDP was above or below trend. The asymmetry hypothesis was not accepted.

6. See table A.1 in the appendix.

7. Exposure to external risk is captured by the share of trade in GDP and a measure of volatility of the terms of trade.

8. While it is possible that the use of public employment varies along the business cycle, expanding during booms, but remaining rigid during recessions, we did not find evidence to support this hypothesis. We tested the hypothesis of asymmetric or ratchet effects in the response of public employment to changes in GDP per capita, with a dummy variable equal to 1 when GDP per capita growth is positive, included by itself and interacted with GDP per capita. We found no significant difference in the response of public employment to changes in GDP along the cycle and hence reject the ratchet effects hypothesis.

9. See all the regions in figure A.2 of the appendix.

10. Table A.3 in the appendix presents the models of determinants of pension payments.

11. Detailed yearly data are presented by Herrera and Velasco (2019) in their background technical paper for this report.

12. This measure has been used amply in the policy analysis of decentralization (Blanco 2017; 2018) as well as in recent academic literature (Eyraud and Lusinyan 2013). This variable measures, for a fixed spending level, the substitution of own revenue for other sources of financing (debt or transfers). It also measures the imbalance between expenditure responsibilities allocated to subnational governments and their capacity to raise own revenues.

13. Higher numbers indicate higher relative power of regional or local governments vis-à-vis the central government.

14. The proxy is defined as current spending minus the wage bill, minus purchases of goods and services, and is discussed by Herrera and Velasco (2019).

15. The efficiency frontier refers to the maximum output level attainable with a given level of input. The efficiency frontier used by Afonso, Schuknecht, and Tanzi (2005, 2010) and Afonso, Romero-Barrutieta, and Monsalve (2013) is estimated by means of data envelopment analysis methods. Public sector output was defined as a composite measure of education, health, infrastructure, administration, equity, and economic performance.

REFERENCES

Alesina, Alberto, Reza Baqir, and William Easterly. 2000. "Redistributive Public Employment." *Journal of Urban Economics* 48 (2): 219–41.

Afonso, António, Alma Romero-Barrutieta, and Emma Monsalve. 2013. "Public Sector Efficiency: Evidence for Latin America." Inter-American Development Bank Discussion Paper 279, Inter-American Development Bank, Washington, DC.

Afonso, António, Ludger Schuknecht, and Vito Tanzi. 2005. "Public Sector Efficiency: An International Comparison." *Public Choice* 123: 321–47.

——. 2010. "Public Sector Efficiency: Evidence for New EU Members States and Emerging Markets." *Applied Economics* 42: 2147–64.

Almeida, Maria Dolores. 2009a. "Rigideces Fiscales en Bolivia." In *Rigideces y Espacios Fiscales en America Latina*, edited by Oscar Cetrángolo and Juan Pablo Jiménez. Serie Documents de Proyectos 269. Santiago: Economic Commission for Latin America and the Caribbean.

——. 2009b. "Rigideces Fiscales en Ecuador." In *Rigideces y Espacios Fiscales en America Latina*, edited by Oscar Cetrángolo and Juan Pablo Jiménez. Serie Documents de Proyectos 269. Santiago: Economic Commission for Latin America and the Caribbean.

Balassa, Bela. 1964. "The Purchasing Power Parity Doctrine: A Reappraisal." *Journal of Political Economy* 72 (6): 584–96.

Bhagwati, Jagdish. 1984. "Why Are Services Cheaper in the Poor Countries?" *Economic Journal* 94 (374): 279–86.

Blanco, F. 2017. "Diagnóstico y Opciones de Reforma del Sistema de Transferencias en la Provincia de Buenos Aires a los Municipios." Unpublished paper, World Bank, Washington, DC.

——. 2018. "Subnational Fiscal Frameworks." Unpublished paper, MTI Forum, World Bank, Washington, DC.

Cabrera, Maynor, and J.A. Fuentes. 2009. "Rigidez Fiscal en Centroamerica: los Casos de Guatemala, Costa Rica, y Honduras." In *Rigideces y Espacios Fiscales en America Latina*, edited by Oscar Cetrángolo and Juan Pablo Jiménez. Serie Documents de Proyectos 269. Santiago: Economic Commission for Latin America and the Caribbean.

Cerda, R., and C. Pessino. 2018. "How Large Are Fiscal Wage Gaps in Latin America? How Can They Be Corrected?" Unpublished paper, Inter-American Development Bank, Washington, DC.

Cetrángolo, Oscar, and Juan Pablo Jiménez. 2009. "Rigideces y Espacios Fiscales en America Latina." Serie Documents de Proyectos 269, Economic Commission for Latin America and the Caribbean, Santiago, Chile.

Cetrángolo, Oscar, Juan Pablo Jiménez, and Ramiro Ruiz del Castillo. 2010. "Rigidities and Fiscal Space in Latin America: A Comparative Case Study." Series Macroeconomía del Desarrollo 97, Economic Commission for Latin America and the Caribbean (ECLAC), Santiago, Chile.

Echeverry, Juan Carlos, Jorge Alexander Bonilla, and Andres Moya. 2006. "Rigideces institucionales y flexibilidad presupuestaria: los casos de Argentina, Colombia, México y Perú." Documento CEDE 2006-33, Universidad de los Andes, Bogotá, Colombia.

Eyraud, Luc, and Lusine Lusinyan. 2013. "Vertical Fiscal Imbalances and Fiscal Performance in Advanced Economies." *Journal of Monetary Economics* 60 (5): 571–87.

Gindling, Thomas, Zahid Hasnain, David Newhouse, and Rong Shi. 2019. "Are Public Sector Workers in Developing Countries Overpaid?" Policy Research Working Paper 8754, World Bank, Washington, DC.

Herrera, S., and E. Munoz. 2019a. "What Determines the Size of Public Employment? An Empirical Investigation." Background Report for Regional Study on Budget Rigidities in Latin America, unpublished paper, World Bank, Washington, DC.

———. 2019b. "Stylized Facts of Budget Rigidity Measures and Fiscal Performance." Background Report for Regional Study on Budget Rigidities in Latin America, unpublished paper, World Bank, Washington, DC.

Herrera, S., and J. Velasco. 2019. "Budget Rigidity in LAC: A Proposed New Measure for Empirical Analysis." Background Report for Regional Study on Budget Rigidities in Latin America, unpublished paper, World Bank, Washington, DC.

IMF (International Monetary Fund). 2016. "Managing Government Compensation and Employment—Institutions, Policies, and Reform Challenges." IMF Policy Paper, Washington, DC.

Izquierdo, Alejandro, Carola Pessino, and Guillermo Vuletin, eds. 2018. *Mejor Gasto para Mejores Vidas*. Washington, DC: Inter-American Development Bank.

Lozano, I. 2000. "Colombia's Public Finance in the 1990s: A Decade of Reforms, Fiscal Imbalance, and Debt." Department of Economic Research. Banco de la Republica, Bogotá, Colombia.

Mattina, Todd, and Victoria Gunnarsson. 2007. "Budget Rigidity and Expenditure Efficiency in Slovenia." IMF Working Paper WP/07/131, International Monetary Fund, Washington, DC.

Rodrik, Dani. 2000. "What Drives Public Employment in Developing Countries?" *Review of Development Economics* 4 (3): 229–43.

Samuelson, P. 1964. "Theoretical Notes on Trade Problems." *Review of Economics and Statistics* 46 (2): 145–54.

Shelton, C. 2007. "The Size and Composition of Government Expenditure." *Journal of Public Economics* 91: 2230–60.

Vegh, Carlos, Luis Morano, Diego Friedheim, and Diego Rojas. 2017. *Between a Rock and a Hard Place: The Monetary Policy Dilemma in Latin America and the Caribbean*. LAC Semiannual Report. Washington, DC: World Bank.

World Bank. 2016. "Chile: Public Expenditure Review." Report 106334-CL, World Bank, Washington, DC.

———. 2017. "A Fair Adjustment: Efficiency and Equity of Public Spending in Brazil." Public Expenditure Review, World Bank, Washington, DC.

4 Policy Implications

Budget rigidities are likely to affect economic performance and lead to suboptimal fiscal outcomes. By preventing the government from conducting appropriate macroeconomic management, budget rigidities can lead to excessive cyclical volatility of the macroeconomy and weaken the sustainability of public debt. Financial markets evaluate the quality of the government as a borrower on the basis of the current and expected future stocks of public debt. If budget rigidities are perceived to prevent the government from reducing budget deficits and generating enough surpluses in the future to compensate for current fiscal expansions, financial markets will downgrade the government's quality rating as a borrower. In other words, as shown by von Hagen and Chen (2019), excessive rigidities worsen the quality of the government's balance sheet, especially during cyclical downturns, and this will increase the government's cost of financing its debt. This section discusses the long-term and short-term effects of budget rigidity on fiscal management, and the policy options to address them. As the Colombia case shows (box 4.1), rigidities can be adjusted in the medium term, and this section discusses the policy options.

RIGIDITIES AND THE GOVERNMENT'S NET WORTH–DEBT SUSTAINABILITY

Sustainability of public finance is a forward-looking concept, and the government's balance sheet should reflect this. Public finance is sustainable if the expected present value of a government's future spending, including debt service, does not exceed the expected present value of its future revenues. Von Hagen and Chen (2019) develop an assessment of the sustainability of public finance, building on a public sector balance sheet approach and then studying the impact of rigidities on sustainability. Critically, their analysis considers what is usually the most important government asset: its power to tax. It also includes potential future primary expenditures derived from contingent liabilities but allows some expenditure to be rigid and not modifiable in the medium term (Chen and von Hagen 2018; von Hagen and Chen 2019).

BOX 4.1

Budget rigidity sources and fiscal policy management in Colombia

At the beginning of the 21st century, a macroeconomic crisis revealed severe budget inflexibilities in Colombia that stemmed from legal, constitutional, and contractual mandates. These budget inflexibilities included unfunded pay-as-you-go pension payments, health care and education expenditures embedded in a subnational government transfer system, and public debt interest payments, among others. The mandates hindered short-run changes in the national government's budget level and composition.

Several consecutive governments developed a full-fledged framework of fiscal policy that helped Colombia weather the 2008 international crisis, the 2009–13 oil price boom, and the 2014–17 oil price collapse. The framework included four channels of budget flexibilization: (a) constitutional and legal reforms reducing the burden of inherited inflexible budget items; (b) public debt and borrowing cost reduction; (c) revenue increases not matched with an expenditure rise; and (d) intrasectoral budget realignments, allowing authorities to reprioritize. These four channels reduced inflexibilities from 95 percent to approximately 75 percent of the Colombian budget (figure B4.1.1). However, budget inflexibility exhibits a pendular movement, and the flexibilizing measures have been undone by increasing social demands for higher-quality education and health care and peace-agreement-related expenditures. Previous analyses studied inflexibilities at the general, national budget level and its broad categories (that is, the operation and investment aggregates). This analysis is the first attempt to analyze the degree of budget flexibility at the ministerial and investment program levels. Fiscal inflexibility is not a curse; it can be cured, but it is bound to resurface, even in the presence of a comprehensive fiscal policy framework, well-accepted fiscal rules, and a managerial community dedicated to enforcing reforms.

FIGURE B4.1.1

Sources of budget rigidities in Colombia, 1994–2016

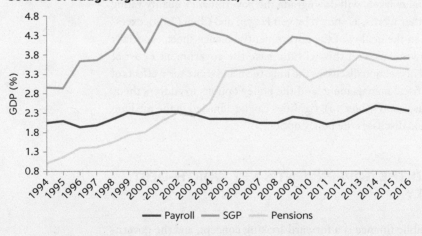

Source: Echeverry 2019.
Note: GDP = gross domestic product; SGP = Sistema General de Participaciones, which is the revenue-sharing mechanism between central government and states and municipalities.

The authors show that, to get a full picture of debt sustainability, it is necessary to evaluate the risk profiles of future revenue and expenditure streams, in addition to their expected present values. Expected present values reflect how revenue and expenditure streams will develop on average or under normal circumstances in the future. But fiscal crises do not occur under normal or average conditions. They occur under special and rare conditions, such as following a large negative shock to tax revenues or a large positive shock to government spending, as many countries experienced in the Great Recession of 2008–09. Following such shocks, it is crucial that governments can return quickly to normal spending and revenue levels, and this is when rigidities become important. With large rigidities, spending and revenue shocks are more likely to push governments into default than with small rigidities. The authors show how rigidities affect the tail risk of government debt (that is, the probability of default under rare and extreme circumstances). Rigidities can have large effects on tail risk even if their effect on expected revenue and expenditure streams is small. Furthermore, the effect of rigidities on sustainability depends on the cyclicality of revenues and expenditures.[1] To protect the government's net worth, taxes should have positive covariance and expenditures negative covariance with the discount factor.

Increased rigidity affects the net present value of expenditures in bad times. Evaluating the government's net worth involves computing the conditional expectations and covariances. This requires modeling the macroeconomy, including the fiscal sector, for individual countries. Von Hagen and Chen did simulations for countries in Latin America and the Caribbean, finding that in general, increased rigidity does not affect the net present value of the different expenditure categories by much, but in bad times, the net worth of the government was significantly affected, as measured by the value at risk.[2]

Estimations done for this report show that a high share of rigidities in the budget can lead countries into fiscal distress by pushing public debt to unsustainable levels (see Munoz and Olaberria 2019). Periods of fiscal distress—identified as periods when either the debt-stabilizing primary balance or the level of public debt are above a certain high threshold—are positively associated with the level of budget rigidities (measured as the share of spending in wages, pensions, and interests), even after controlling for economic and political factors that previous literature has identified as potential determinants of this probability (see table A.5 in the appendix and Muñoz and Olaberria 2019 for details).

RIGIDITIES AND THE ABILITY TO PERFORM FISCAL ADJUSTMENT

A key motivation for this report is the question of whether a high share of budget rigidities can push countries into fiscal distress and diminish the likelihood of a government carrying out fiscal consolidation. Conceptually, it is clear how budget rigidities can increase the probability of countries getting into fiscal distress and constrain the ability of governments to consolidate. Political economy theory emphasizes that government spending often increases because relevant expenditure items are rigid as a result of entitlements or indexation to economic variables that are outside the control of the government (Alesina, Perotti, and Tavares 1998). This way, expenditures cannot be modified during the annual decision-making process over the public budget. These can be very important sources of the loss of control of fiscal policy that can get countries into fiscal distress. Similarly, indications are widespread that Latin American countries face tough political battles when trying to implement fiscal adjustments that involve cutting public wages or social benefits. For example, in December 2017, Argentina's lower house had to suspend a vote on President Mauricio Macri's pension reform plan (which hoped to limit the growth rate of pensions) after the debate became a shouting match and protesters and police clashed violently outside Congress. However, other countries have been able to implement large fiscal adjustments even under strong political pressure, such as Uruguay in the early 2000s (see box 4.2).

Fiscal adjustment in the presence of budget rigidities in Uruguay, 2002–05

The Uruguayan experience of fiscal adjustment shows that the rigidity of spending can be significantly reduced in times of crisis, but not without social and political costs. Between 1999 and 2004, there was a sharp contraction in total expenditures of the central government as part of the adjustment implemented to deal with the fiscal and financial difficulties arising from the 2002 crisis. In a period of just five years, the government achieved a drastic decrease in primary expenditure of almost 5 percentage points of GDP (figure B4.2.1).

The strong compression of primary spending in this short period of time was possible under exceptional circumstances. It is likely that, without a consensus among political actors on the complexity of public finance, the adjustment process would not have been possible. This shows that in extreme situations, conditions can be generated to make important cuts in primary expenditure components that, in principle, should be considered extremely rigid.

The fiscal adjustment, together with the rescheduling of the maturity of the public debt carried out in 2003, was implemented within the framework of a stand-by program with the International Monetary Fund that allowed the government to cover most of its needs. This financing was provided in a context in which the international capital markets were not willing to provide the necessary funds, not even for the rollover of debt maturities. The main objective of the adjustment program was to reduce the fiscal deficit to a sustainable level (see figure B4.2.1).

The strong adjustment of primary expenditure aimed to compensate for the increase in interest expenditure of 3 percent of GDP, which was due to the significant growth of public debt after the strong nominal and real devaluation that occurred in 2002. By the end of 2004, the interest payment on the public debt had increased to almost 6 percentage points of GDP, significantly higher than the 2 percent of GDP that was the average during the years prior to the crisis. The increase in the interest payment became, in fact, a significant element of rigidity in public finance that forced the authorities that took office in March 2005 to maintain levels of primary surplus of between 3 and 4 percent of GDP for several years.

FIGURE B4.2.1

General government revenues, expenditures, and primary deficit in Uruguay, 1999–2010

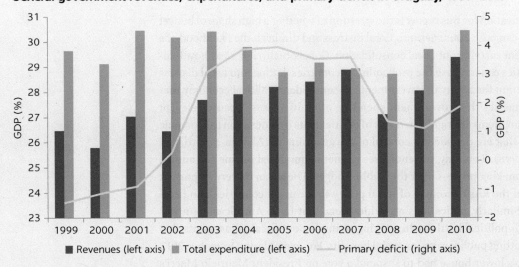

■ Revenues (left axis)　■ Total expenditure (left axis)　—— Primary deficit (right axis)

Source: Lorenzo 2018.

To provide a rigorous answer to this question, it is critical to clearly identify periods of fiscal need. In a technical background paper produced for this report, Muñoz and Olaberria (2019) assume that when any country is facing an objective need for fiscal adjustment, the government will attempt to do so; if it does not do so, it is because of institutional, economic, or political factors that constrain the government's ability. For this hypothesis to be reasonable, the fiscal need must be clear and pressing. Muñoz and Olaberria identify episodes of fiscal adjustment need using two different approaches. First, they follow Escolano et al. (2014) to define fiscal adjustment needs as years in which a country is facing a positive primary gap for two consecutive years greater or equal than an arbitrary threshold (see their paper for more details). Second, they consider the case of countries with the ratio of public debt over average revenue above a country-specific rolling Gaussian weighted average for two consecutive years. Periods of fiscal adjustment are identified as consecutive years in which there is an improvement of at least 0.1 percent of gross domestic product (GDP) in the cyclically adjusted primary balance. Their probability of occurrence is negatively correlated with the level of budget rigidities (see table A.6 in the appendix). Then, Muñoz and Olaberria (2019) apply a linear probability model to a set of 182 advanced and developing countries.

A key finding is that relatively high shares of rigid (observed) components of public spending contribute to countries getting into fiscal distress and are a constraint on fiscal consolidation. The authors find evidence that a relatively high share of nonstructural rigid spending contributes to the probability of fiscal distress and reduces the probability of fiscal consolidation. Moreover, the effect of rigid expenditure seems to be more relevant for economies with high inequality, governments with lower margins of majority, and countries with lower institutional quality. In addition, when looking at the composition of the measure of rigid expenditure, there is evidence that higher expenditure on pensions reduce the probability of fiscal adjustment more robustly than higher expenditure on wages.

RIGIDITIES AND THE CYCLICALITY OF FISCAL POLICY

Latin American countries have not generated enough fiscal savings because their fiscal policy has been consistently among the most procyclical in the world (Vegh et al. 2017). Procyclical fiscal policy means that public spending growth is expansionary (higher than it should be) in good times and contractionary (lower than it should be) during bad times, reinforcing the business cycle, increasing households' income volatility, and reducing welfare. It goes against standard Keynesian prescriptions that would call for exactly the opposite policies: be expansionary (spend relatively more) to stimulate the economy in bad times and cool it down in good times. This misguided procyclical fiscal policy has been followed in Latin America for several decades.

Fiscal procyclicality can be the result of several factors. The first generation of research papers highlighted the lack of access to credit and international capital markets to explain such behavior, with the seminal contribution of Gavin and Perotti (1997) focusing on Latin American countries. The second generation of papers, as illustrated by Talvi and Vegh (2005), examined the role of political distortions, and particularly political polarization, to explain the "voracity effects" on the budget during booms. This explanation was found to be the most relevant empirically (Ilzetzki 2011). Alesina, Campante, and Tabellini (2008) showed that higher perceived levels of corruption (especially with a lack of fiscal transparency) led to a rational decision of the voters to "starve the Leviathan," that is, to reduce political rents by demanding more public goods (and/or lower taxes) during booms. More recent developments in the literature have examined the resource-led boom of many developed economies and concluded that procyclical behavior was stronger in resource-dependent nations (Arezki and Brückner 2012, with further examination and a focus on Sub-Saharan Africa by Konuki and Villafuerte 2016). This section analyzes whether budget rigidity also exacerbates the procyclical behavior of fiscal policy.

Procyclicality is associated with perceptions of corruption, social fragmentation, inequality in resource distribution, a lower quality of fiscal institutions, and inadequate fiscal rules. The main economic variables that affect procyclicality are financial depth, tax base variability, and natural resource dependence, as well as inequality. In line with the political economy literature, this report finds that the perception of corruption is positively associated with procyclicality, as are social fragmentation and inequality in resource distribution. Similarly, the report shows that the political cycle affects procyclicality, as the procyclical bias increases in electoral years (Herrera, Kouame, and Mandon 2019).

More rigid spending is associated with a lower degree of procyclicality, but the effect is not symmetric along the business cycle; the dampening effect on the procyclical bias is more pronounced during booms, which can be interpreted as a positive effect (von Hagen and Chen 2019). Countries with fiscal rules have smaller procyclical bias, but the effect is not homogeneous: fiscal rules with clauses on the sustainability of policies or estimations of the costs of measures are associated with countercyclicality; fiscal councils are also associated with a countercyclical fiscal stance.

RIGIDITIES AND THE EFFICIENCY OF PUBLIC SPENDING

Efficiency of government expenditures relates to the extent to which the government achieves its policy goals with a given amount of resources. Expenditures are more efficient if they reach the intended goals to a greater degree. Tanzi (1998), Tanzi and Schuknecht (2000), and Afonso, Schuknecht, and Tanzi (2005) explain the concept of expenditure efficiency and develop efficiency measures based on models of production functions for public sector services.

Rigidities can reflect the government's commitment to certain policies and their related expenditures. Such a commitment is often necessary to induce private citizens to engage in desirable activities such as education and training. When public funding for education and training programs is highly volatile, citizens will not invest time and their own resources in them, fearing that the programs may be stopped suddenly before they have a chance to complete them and reap the benefits. More generally, in areas in which the achievement of policy goals requires the cooperation of the government and private citizens or institutions, commitment and, therefore, rigidity, are necessary for a high degree of efficiency.

However, rigidities can also reduce the government's ability to react to changing circumstances and demand for public services. For example, a rule fixing the level or ratio of public expenditures for physical infrastructure may lead to a situation in which the government funds infrastructure projects with low marginal returns rather than programs in greater demand, such as health or education.

Given the ambiguous relationship between rigidity and efficiency of government expenditures, they must be evaluated together for individual types of government expenditures. This can be achieved by integrating performance measures for different government programs into the budget process, such as by performing regular expenditure reviews that evaluate government policies, or by introducing elements of performance budgeting into the budget process (Curristine, Lonti, and Joumard 2007).

NOTES

1. Technically, the authors show that the present value of a stream of revenues will be higher if the covariance of revenues and the discount factor is positive. Recall that the discount factor depends on the ratio of current consumption to expected future consumption. If expected future consumption is higher than the current level, then the utility of future consumption will be lower, and discounted at a higher rate. Hence, the sustainability of public finance requires that future economic consumption and output be positively associated with public revenues. On the expenditure side, if household future consumption is expected to be high, then expected government spending should be low to maintain the overall economy's budget constraint. The covariance between expenditures and discount rates should be negative. In standard microeconomic and applied welfare analysis, it is shown that if the utility function is of the constant relative risk aversion (CRRA) type, there is an equilibrium condition that establishes a relationship between the rate of discount (r), the growth rate of consumption (g), the rate of time preference (ρ), and the risk aversion parameter (θ), such that $r = \rho + \theta g$. This is the framework used in the *Stern Review* of the economics of climate change (with $\rho = .1\%$, $g = 2\%$, and $\theta = 1\%$) (see Stern 2006). See Gollier (2011) for a synthesis. This relationship between the rate of discount and the growth rate of consumption has been used in countries in Latin America and the Caribbean by Lopez (2008).
2. Von Hagen and Chen (2019) measure rigidity by the persistence coefficient in vector autoregressions. It is a different measure of rigidity than is used in the other background technical papers.

REFERENCES

Afonso, António, Ludger Schuknecht, and Vito Tanzi. 2005. "Public Sector Efficiency: An International Comparison." *Public Choice* 123: 321–47.

Alesina, Alberto, F. Campante, and G. Tabellini. 2008. "Why Is Fiscal Policy Often Procyclical?" *Journal of the European Economic Association* 6: 1006–36.

Alesina, Alberto, Roberto Perotti, and Jose Tavares. 1998. "The Political Economy of Fiscal Adjustments." *Brookings Papers on Economic Activity*, 1: 197–266. doi:10.2307/2534672.

Arezki, Rabah, and Markus Brückner. 2012. "Commodity Windfalls, Democracy and External Debt." *Economic Journal* 122 (561): 848–66.

Chen, Yao, and Jürgen von Hagen. 2018. "Fiscal Risk and Public Sector Balance Sheets." Working Paper, University of Bonn, and ADEMU Working Paper 2018/113, Bonn and Barcelona.

Curristine, Teresa, Zsuzsanna Lonti, and Isabelle Joumard. 2007. "Improving Public Sector Efficiency: Challenges and Opportunities." *OECD Journal on Budgeting* 7 (1): 1–41.

Echeverry, Juan Carlos. 2019. "Combating Budget Inflexibility in Colombia 2000–2016." Background Report for Regional Study on Budget Rigidities in Latin America." Unpublished paper, World Bank, Washington, DC.

Escolano, J., L. Jaramillo, C. Mulas-Granados, and G. Terrier. 2014. "How Much Is a Lot? Historical Evidence on the Size of Fiscal Adjustments." IMF Working Paper 14/179, International Monetary Fund, Washington, DC.

Gavin, Michael, and Roberto Perotti. 1997. "Fiscal Policy in Latin America." In *NBER Macroeconomics Annual 1997, Volume 12*, edited by Ben Bernanke and Julio Rotemberg. Cambridge, MA: MIT Press.

Gollier, C. 2011. *Pricing the Future: The Economics of Discounting and Sustainable Development.* Princeton, NJ: Princeton University Press.

Herrera, Santiago, Wilfred Kouame, and Pierre Mandon. 2019. "Why Some Countries Can Escape the Fiscal Pro-cyclicality Trap and Others Can't." Background Report for Regional Study on Budget Rigidities in Latin America, unpublished paper, World Bank, Washington, DC.

Ilzetzki, Ethan. 2011. "Rent-Seeking Distortions and Fiscal Procyclicality." *Journal of Development Economics* 96 (1): 30–46.

Konuki, Tetsuya, and Mauricio Villafuerte. 2016. "Cyclical Behavior of Fiscal Policy among Sub-Saharan African Countries." Working paper, International Monetary Fund, African Department, Washington, DC.

Lopez, H. 2008. "The Social Discount Rate: Estimates for Nine Latin American Countries." Policy Research Working Paper 4639, World Bank, Washington, DC.

Lorenzo, F. 2018. "Rigideces Presupuestales en Uruguay." Background Report for Regional Study on Budget Rigidities in Latin America, unpublished paper, World Bank, Washington, DC.

Muñoz, Erico, and Eduardo Olaberria. 2019. "Are Budget Rigidities a Source of Fiscal Distress and a Constraint for Fiscal Consolidation?" Policy Research Working Paper Series 8957, World Bank, Washington, DC. https://openknowledge.worldbank.org/handle/10986/32209.

Stern, Nicholas. 2006. *The Economics of Climate Change: The Stern Review.* London: U.K. Chancellor of the Exchequer. http://mudancasclimaticas.cptec.inpe.br/~rmclima/pdfs/destaques/sternreview_report_complete.pdf.

Talvi, Ernesto, and Carlos Vegh. 2005. "Tax Base Variability and Procyclical Fiscal Policy in Developing Countries." *Journal of Development Economics* 78 (1): 156–90.

Tanzi, Vito. 1998. "Government Role and the Efficiency of Policy Instruments." In *Public Finance in a Changing World*, edited by Peter Birch Sorensen, 51–69. London: Palgrave Macmillan.

Tanzi, Vito, and Ludger Schuknecht. 2000. *Public Spending in the 20th Century: A Global Perspective.* Cambridge: Cambridge University Press.

Vegh, Carlos, Daniel Lederman, Federico Bennett, and Samuel Pienknagura. 2017. *Leaning Against the Wind: Fiscal Policy in Latin America and the Caribbean in a Historical Perspective.* Washington, DC: World Bank Group.

von Hagen, Jürgen, and Yao Chen. 2019. "Budget Rigidities and Fiscal Performance in Latin America and the Caribbean." Background Report for Regional Study on Budget Rigidities in Latin America, unpublished paper, World Bank, Washington, DC.

5 Conclusion

This report has presented a new measure of expenditure rigidity that can be easily applied to a large set of countries and that allows tracking of the problem over time; the report has also examined the measure's implications for fiscal performance. The report finds that a high level of budget rigidity has important impacts on fiscal performance: it increases the country's financing needs; it increases the probability of a country getting into fiscal distress and reduces the ability to start fiscal adjustment; and it is associated with more inefficient levels of public spending, which reduces the quality of public services and, therefore, the welfare of the population. Higher rigidity levels are also associated with higher debt and higher taxes rates.

This new measure of rigidity is based on the decomposition of public spending into two components: a structural component that is determined by long-run economic fundamentals, and a nonstructural component that is determined by policy decisions or short-run effects of variables associated with the business cycle. The structural component is determined by long-run economic, demographic, and institutional fundamentals beyond the policy maker's control, and will be interpreted as the rigid level of spending.[1] The nonstructural component is the difference between the observed level and the structural one, and it is determined by short-run transitory factors related to the business or political cycles. The degree of rigidity of spending is approximated by the ratio of structural spending to total spending. The non-structural component of wages or pension payments provides an indication of the discretion that policy makers have used in the past, causing deviations of total spending from the structural level.

Rigidities play a critical role in determining how a country can recover from economic shocks. Following such shocks, it is crucial that governments can return quickly to normal spending and revenue levels, and this is where rigidities become important. With large rigidities, spending and revenue shocks are more likely to push governments into default than with small rigidities. The authors show how rigidities affect the tail risk of government debt (that is, the probability of default under rare and extreme circumstances). Rigidities can have large effects on tail risk even if their effect on expected revenue and expenditure streams is small. Furthermore, the effect of rigidities on sustainability depends on the cyclicality of revenues and expenditures. To protect the government's net worth, taxes should have positive covariance and expenditures negative covariance with the discount factor.

A main conclusion is that many countries in Latin American need to (and can) tackle rigid expenditures to be able to adjust public finance and put their debts on a sustainable path. This calls for urgent action, as many countries in the region are facing worrisome fiscal challenges due to surging debt-to-GDP ratios. Given low inflation levels, which prevent governments from using inflation to reduce the debt in real terms, and large infrastructure gaps (due to historically low capital spending), which prevent governments from adjusting public investment, governments have no choice but to reduce the more rigid components of spending.

Latin American countries potentially have more room to reduce rigid expenditure. This report finds that budget rigidity is not a phenomenon exclusive to Latin America and the Caribbean; on the contrary, other regions face higher levels of rigid expenditure. However, this has not prevented countries in other regions from implementing successful consolidation plans. In Latin America, the nonstructural component of rigid expenditure tends to be higher than in other regions, which gives policy makers more room to act, as it is subject to policy makers' discretion.

The report has also presented historical evidence showing that rigid components of spending can be reduced when there is the political will to do so. The case studies of Colombia and Uruguay prove this. A good framework for budget flexibilization in the short term should include the following dimensions: (a) constitutional and legal reforms reducing the burden of inherited inflexible budget items; (b) improvements in debt management to reduce borrowing cost reduction; (c) revenue increases not matched with an expenditure rise; and (d) intrasectoral budget realignments, allowing authorities to reprioritize.

Policy makers' battle against budget rigidities must be a long-term process to contain the sources of rigidity. The main elements of such a strategy include the following actions:

- Continue and deepen the pension reform process. This would entail increasing the retirement age and facilitating private sector participation in the pension funds sector, which would increase the options for individuals to save for retirement in their individual accounts. In addition, increasing the labor market participation of women would increase the ratio of contributing workers in pay-as-you-go systems.
- Develop fiscal institutions that promote medium-term fiscal planning and incorporate the costs of any wage increase time—for example, a congressional budget office and a medium-term fiscal framework that is approved by an external committee. In Chile, the copper price for the budget and the cyclically adjusted GDP are determined by independent technical committees. Such committees should ensure that wage increases keep pace with the productivity of the overall economy.
- Delegate more technical assessments to fiscal councils to reduce the transaction costs of the budget negotiation process. Drawing on the association between fiscal councils and countercyclical policy management, more delegation should be given to such councils to decide on long-term budget composition matters, such as the wage bill over the long run.

The fiscal council would limit the role of nonstructural factors in the evolution of the wage bill.

- Enhance transparency in the budget. This will reduce the need for spending floors or spending rules to ensure allocation of resources to specific activities. If information on the budget (expenditures and revenues) is produced on a timely and reliable basis following international standards, the transaction costs of budget negotiation will be reduced.
- Reduce budget fragmentation. Giving the complete picture of public resource allocation and distribution allows for a more expedient budget approval process that can change as circumstances change.
- Limit earmarking and provide exit clauses to existing constitutional spending mandates. The policy maker should have discretion in the case of fiscal imbalances. Fiscal medium-term sustainability could be granted prevalence over other policy objectives such as redistribution.
- Create room for fiscal maneuvering from the planning stage. New spending must come with its own revenues, and social obligations and commitments must be subject to sustainability constraints.

NOTE

1. This estimation of the long-run or structural relationships is based on panel data for up to 166 countries from 1980 to 2017. Data availability varies for each type of spending, so it considers both individual country and cross-country relationships between the variables.

Estimation of the Structural Component of Spending

This study estimates rigid expenditure by adding structural public wages, structural pensions payments, and actual interest payments. The structural component of the subnational government (SNG) transfers are not included to avoid double counting of transfers to pay for salaries, mostly of education and health sectors. The SNG structural component is presented because of its significance as a source of rigidity for some countries, such as Brazil, Colombia, Mexico, and Peru.

$$\begin{matrix} Rigid \\ Expenditure \end{matrix} = \begin{matrix} Structural \\ public\ wages \end{matrix} + \begin{matrix} Structural \\ pension\ payments \end{matrix} + \begin{matrix} Interest \\ payments \end{matrix}$$

The structurally rigid expenditure is estimated using a fixed-effect model in which the logarithm of the expenditure per capita in constant international dollars ($y_{i,j}$) depends on a set of structural independent variables ($x_{i,j}$), such as the logarithm of GDP per capita in constant international dollars, the logarithm of the population, or the dependency ratios, among others. The fixed effects (u_i) absorb the time-invariant structural heterogeneity across countries, and the structural covariates capture the variation in expenditure explained by changes of structural factors over time. The residuals ($\varepsilon_{i,j}$), are the difference between observed spending levels and the structural component. The estimated functions are displaced, such that all residuals are positive, following the corrected ordinary least square (COLS) method:[1]

$$\ln(y_{i,j}) = Ax_{i,j} + u_i + \varepsilon_{i,j}$$

The scatter plot in figure A.1 illustrates this procedure. The solid line is the part of the model that is defined by time-variant structural factors, the logarithm of GDP per capita in this illustration. The dashed line is a country-specific estimation that includes the effect of time-variant structural factors and country time-invariant characteristics. The difference between these two lines, the fixed effects, captures the structural heterogeneities across countries resulting from unobservable time-invariant characteristics.

Estimation of structural expenditure (corrected least square approach)

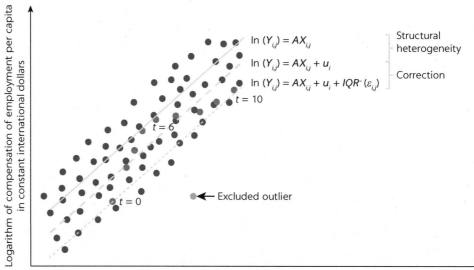

TABLE A.1 **Determinants of general government employment**

VARIABLE	(1)	(2)	(3)	(4)	(5)	(6)
Log of population	−0.147***	−0.130***	−0.137***	−0.138***	−0.143***	−0.138***
	(0.029)	(0.029)	(0.032)	(0.035)	(0.035)	(0.036)
Log of GDP per capita	0.239***	0.223**	0.222	0.275**	0.226	0.250
	(0.076)	(0.093)	(0.139)	(0.108)	(0.189)	(0.195)
Openness	−0.190***	0.217	0.195	0.179	−0.077	0.155
	(0.072)	(0.224)	(0.220)	(0.275)	(0.293)	(0.251)
Ethnic fractionaliza-tion	−0.739***	−0.607**	−0.617**	−0.465		−0.462
	(0.269)	(0.267)	(0.280)	(0.330)		(0.321)
High income		0.490*	0.472*	0.433	0.333	0.430
		(0.285)	(0.280)	(0.367)	(0.379)	(0.349)
High income * openness		−0.448**	−0.413*	−0.463*	−0.233	−0.437*
		(0.211)	(0.213)	(0.262)	(0.280)	(0.249)
Age depen-dency ratio, young			−0.001		−0.007	−0.002
			(0.005)		(0.007)	(0.008)
Age depen-dency ratio, old			−0.003		−0.003	−0.001
			(0.005)		(0.007)	(0.007)
Gini				0.002	0.003	0.003
				(0.008)	(0.010)	(0.011)
Constant	0.904	0.587	0.718	0.058	0.819	0.376
	(0.743)	(0.795)	(1.439)	(0.801)	(1.616)	(1.751)
Observations	286	286	284	223	224	223
Number of countries	80	80	79	72	73	72
Country FE	No	No	No	No	No	No
R^2	0.347	0.355	0.358	0.352	0.372	0.351

Source: Herrera and Munoz 2019.
Note: Robust standard errors clustered by country in parentheses. FE = fixed effects.
Significance level: *** $p < 0.01$, ** $p < 0.05$, * $p < 0.1$.

TABLE A.2 **Structural determinants of public wages**

DEPENDENT VARIABLE: LOG OF PUBLIC WAGE BILL PER CAPITA, CONSTANT INTERNATIONAL DOLLARS	
Logarithm of the GDP per capita, constant international dollars	1.187***
	(0.0251)
Logarithm of population	0.165***
	(0.0393)
Population density, people per sq. km of land area	−0.000152***
	(3.82e-05)
Urban population, percent of total	0.00737***
	(0.00180)
Young age dependency ratio, percent of working-age population	0.00665***
	(0.000820)
Old age dependency ratio, percent of working-age population	−0.00694**
	(0.00300)
Openness, percent of GDP	−0.000952***
	(0.000235)
Constant	−7.459***
	(0.640)
Observations	3,369
Number of countries	153
R^2	0.520
F-test	497.5
sigma_u	0.646
sigma_e	0.213
Rho	0.902
Minimum observations per group	1
Average observations per group	22.02
Maximum observations per group	28

Source: Herrera and Velasco 2019.
Note: Standard errors in parentheses.
Significance level: *** $p < 0.01$, ** $p < 0.05$, * $p < 0.1$.

This model is corrected to have only positive errors by shifting it "downward" by the minimum error. This procedure is equivalent to an estimate of a frontier that defines the minimum expenditure possible given the countries' structural characteristics. The errors are first cleaned for outliers, eliminating those that exceed 1.5 times the interquartile range (IQR):[2]

$$\ln(\hat{y}_{i,j}) = Ax_{i,j} + u_i + \text{IRQ}^-(\varepsilon_{i,j})$$

The dotted line in figure A.1 represents the corrected model that describes structural expenditure that used to be below actual spending. In the particular case represented by the orange dots, actual spending was close to its structural level in year zero ($t = 0$), suggesting that it would be difficult to adjust. However, in the sixth year ($t = 6$) actual expenditure is significantly higher than its structural component, and hence it would be easier to adjust.

FIGURE A.2

Deviation of observed public employment from predicted levels, based on fundamentals as a percentage of the labor force (95% confidence interval)

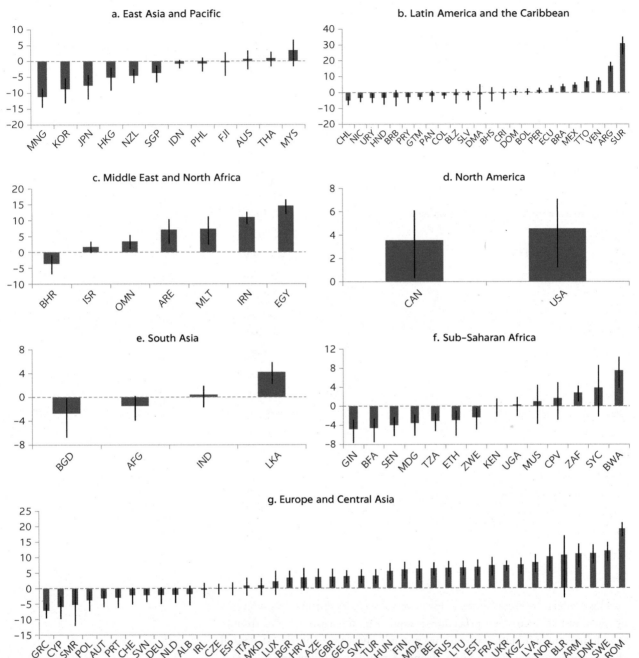

Source: Herrera and Munoz 2019.

Note: The prediction model is log(E/LF) = −1.38 − .11*log(Population) + .10*log(GDPPC) + .11*Openness − .56*Ethnic + .47*High Income − .27*High Income*Openness.

AFG = Afghanistan; ALB = Albania; ARE = United Arab Emirates; ARG = Argentina; ARM = Armenia; AUS = Australia; AUT = Austria; AZE = Azerbaijan; BEL = Belgium; BFA = Burkina Faso; BGD = Bangladesh; BGR = Bulgaria; BHR = Bahrain; BHS = The Bahamas; BLR = Belarus; BLZ = Belize; BOL = Bolivia; BRA = Brazil; BRB = Barbados; BWA = Botswana; CAN = Canada; CHE = Switzerland; CHL = Chile; COL = Colombia; CPV = Cabo Verde; CRI = Costa Rica; CYP = Cyprus; CZE = Czech Republic; DEU = Germany; DMA = Dominica; DNK = Denmark; DOM = Dominican Republic; ECU = Ecuador; EGY = Arab Republic of Egypt; ESP = Spain; EST = Estonia; ETH = Ethiopia; FIN = Finland; FJI = Fiji; FRA = France; GBR = United Kingdom; GEO = Georgia; GIN = Guinea; GRC = Greece; GTM = Guatemala; HKG = Hong Kong SAR, China; HND = Honduras; HRV = Croatia; HUN = Hungary; IDN = Indonesia; IND = India; IRL = Ireland; IRN = Islamic Republic of Iran; ISR = Israel; ITA = Italy; JPN = Japan; KEN = Kenya; KGZ = Kyrgyz Republic; KOR = Republic of Korea; LKA = Sri Lanka; LTU = Lithuania; LUX = Luxembourg; LVA = Latvia; MDA = Moldova; MDG = Madagascar; MEX = Mexico; MKD = North Macedonia; MLT = Malta; MNG = Mongolia; MYS = Malaysia; MUS = Mauritius; NIC = Nicaragua; NLD = Netherlands; NOR = Norway; NZL = New Zealand; OMN = Oman; PAN = Panama; PER = Peru; PHL = Philippines; POL = Poland; PRT = Portugal; PRY = Paraguay; ROM = Romania; RUS = Russian Federation; SEN = Senegal; SGP = Singapore; SLV = El Salvador; SMR = San Marino; SUR = Suriname; SVK = Slovak Republic; SVN = Slovenia; SWE = Sweden; SYC = Seychelles; THA = Thailand; TTO = Trinidad and Tobago; TUR = Turkey; TZA = Tanzania; UGA = Uganda; UKR = Ukraine; URY = Uruguay; USA = United States; VEN = Venezuela, RB; ZAF = South Africa; ZWE = Zimbabwe.

TABLE A.3 **Structural determinants of the log of social security benefits per capita, constant international dollars**

Log of the GDP per capita, constant international dollars	0.552***
	(0.0528)
Log of social security revenues per capita, constant international dollars	0.322***
	(0.0317)
Log of population	1.093***
	(0.119)
Population density, people per sq. km of land area	0.0155***
	(0.00350)
Labor force participation rate, percent of total population ages 15+	−0.0230***
	(0.00445)
Constant	−17.18***
	(1.751)
Observations	1,309
Number of countries	62
R^2	0.496
F-test	244.7
sigma_u	1.889
sigma_e	0.253
Rho	0.982
Minimum observations per group	6
Average observations per group	21.11
Maximum observations per group	28

Source: Herrera and Velasco 2019.

TABLE A.4 **Structural determinants of the logarithm of central government transfers to subnational governments**

The logarithm of the GDP per capita, constant international dollars	0.849***
	(0.0728)
The logarithm of tax revenues of subnational per capita, constant international dollars	0.299***
	(0.0426)
Vertical imbalance	0.00966***
	(0.00323)
Equal distribution of resources index (v2xeg_eqdr)	−0.298
	(0.534)
Division of power index (v2x_feduni)	0.857***
	(0.170)
Interaction between v2xeg_eqdr and v2x_feduni	0.0199***
	(0.00443)
Constant	−5.229***
	(0.805)

continued

TABLE A.4, *continued*

Observations	969
Number of countries	69
R^2	0.531
F-test	1
sigma_u	14.04
sigma_e	27
Rho	0.531
Minimum observations per group	0.854
Average observations per group	0.828
Maximum observations per group	168.7

Source: Herrera and Velasco 2019.
Note: Standard errors in parentheses.
Significance level: *** $p < 0.01$, ** $p < 0.05$, * $p < 0.1$.

TABLE A.5 Rigidity and probability of fiscal need

DEPENDENT VARIABLE: NEED FOR FISCAL ADJUSTMENT, BASED ON ESCOLANO ET AL. (2014)								
VARIABLE	**(1)**	**(2)**	**(3)**	**(4)**	**(5)**	**(6)**	**(7)**	**(8)**
Rigid expenditure	0.037***	0.033***	0.038***	0.032***	0.041***	0.033***	0.021	0.028***
(% of GDP)	(0.006)	(0.005)	(0.006)	(0.005)	(0.007)	(0.010)	(0.013)	(0.009)
Economic factors								
GDP growth (*t*-1)		−1 928***		−1.829***	−1.749***	−1.824***	−1.820***	−1.841***
		(0.413)		(0.420)	(0.409)	(0.424)	(0.416)	(0.424)
Inflation (*t*-1)		−0.090		−0.053	−0.049	−0.053	−0.051	−0.056
		(0.074)		(0.066)	(0.062)	(0.066)	(0.067)	(0.067)
U.S. Interest rate		−0.012		−0.015	−0.017	−0.015	−0.017	−0.015
		(0.010)		(0.011)	(0.011)	(0.011)	(0.011)	(0.011)
Political factors								
Gini			0.007	0.005	0.005	0.006	0.005	0.005
			(0.005)	(0.005)	(0.005)	(0.007)	(0.005)	(0.005)
Rule of law			0.002	0.012	0.004	0.012	−0.053	0.013
			(0.029)	(0.030)	(0.029)	(0.030)	(0.050)	(0.030)
Margin of majority			0.092	0.059	0.066	0.059	0.063	−0.094
			(0.123)	(0.124)	(0.124)	(0.124)	(0.125)	(0.231)
Election year			0.021	0.028*	0.029**	0.028*	0.028*	0.028*
			(0.015)	(0.015)	(0.015)	(0.015)	(0.015)	(0.015)
Interactions								
EMEs * Rigidity					−0.017*			
					(0.010)			
Gini * Rigidity						−0.000		
						(0.000)		
Rule of law * Rigidit							0.002	
							(0.002)	

continued

TABLE A.5, *continued*

DEPENDENT VARIABLE: NEED FOR FISCAL ADJUSTMENT, BASED ON ESCOLANO ET AL. (2014)								
VARIABLE	(1)	(2)	(3)	(4)	(5)	(6)	(7)	(8)
Majority * Rigidity								0.007
								(0.012)
Constant	−0.840***	−0.607***	−1.212***	−0.884***	−0.874***	−0.913**	−0.618*	−0.796***
	(0.163)	(0.136)	(0.308)	(0.277)	(0.275)	(0.346)	(0.327)	(0.297)
Observations	1,521	1,500	1,360	1,342	1,342	1,342	1,342	1,342
R^2	0.126	0.182	0.139	0.186	0.193	0.186	0.188	0.187
Number of countries	84	84	75	75	75	75	75	75
Country FE	Yes	Yes	Yes	Yes	Yes	Yes	Yes	Yes

Source: Munoz and Olaberria 2019.
Note: Robust standard errors clustered by country in parentheses. EME = emerging market economy; FE = fixed effects.
Significance level: *** $p < 0.01$, ** $p < 0.05$, * $p < 0.1$.

TABLE A.6 **Rigidity and probability of fiscal adjustment**

DEPENDENT VARIABLE: FISCAL ADJUSTMENT WHEN NEEDED BASED ON ESCOLANO ET AL. (2014)								
VARIABLE	(1)	(2)	(3)	(4)	(5)	(6)	(7)	(8)
Rigid expenditure	−0.014	−0.023***	−0.014	−0.027***	−0.016*	0.073**	−0.080***	−0.062***
(% of GDP)	(0.014)	(0.008)	(0.013)	(0.008)	(0.008)	(0.028)	(0.028)	(0.019)
Economic factors								
GDP growth (t-1)		−0.043		0.479	0.520	0.443	0.400	0.436
		(1.337)		(1.418)	(1.392)	(1.393)	(1.419)	(1.416)
Inflation (t-1)		2.500***		2.721**	3.068***	2.991***	3.219***	2.570**
		(0.844)		(1.098)	(1.114)	(1.084)	(1.000)	(1.173)
U.S. interest rate		−0.122**		−0.157**	−0.175**	−0.204***	−0.192**	−0.172***
		(0.051)		(0.063)	(0.072)	(0.059)	(0.072)	(0.051)
Political factors								
Gini			0.010	0.012	0.014	0.079***	0.014	0.005
			(0.010)	(0.012)	(0.012)	(0.023)	(0.012)	(0.011)
Rule of law			−0.214***	0.091	0.140	0.160	−0.124	0.090
			(0.068)	(0.131)	(0.146)	(0.133)	(0.127)	(0.132)
Margin of majority			0.516	0.250	0.236	0.451	0.243	−1.486*
			(0.406)	(0.385)	(0.379)	(0.360)	(0.375)	(0.800)
Election year			−0.111	−0.093	−0.085	−0.074	−0.084	−0.079
			(0.081)	(0.078)	(0.075)	(0.074)	(0.078)	(0.081)
Interactions								
EMEs * Rigidity					−0.032			
					(0.029)			
Gini * Rigidity						−0.003***		
						(0.001)		

continued

TABLE A.6, *continued*

DEPENDENT VARIABLE: FISCAL ADJUSTMENT WHEN NEEDED BASED ON ESCOLANO ET AL. (2014)								
VARIABLE	(1)	(2)	(3)	(4)	(5)	(6)	(7)	(8)
Rule of law * Rigidy							0.012**	
							(0.005)	
Majority * Rigidity								0.072*
								(0.041)
Constant	0.611	1.167***	0.758	0.456	0.349	−2.486**	1.414	1.601*
	(0.393)	(0.288)	(0.675)	(0.923)	(0.860)	(1.225)	(0.910)	(0.931)
Observations	185	183	165	163	163	163	163	163
R^2	0.007	0.114	0.073	0.159	0.167	0.191	0.177	0.187
Number of countries	60	60	53	53	53	53	53	53
Country FE	Yes	Yes	Yes	Yes	Yes	Yes	Yes	Yes

Source: Munoz and Olaberria 2019.
Note: Robust standard errors clustered by country in parentheses. EME = emerging market economy; FE = fixed effects.
Significance level: *** $p < 0.01$, ** $p < 0.05$, * $p < 0.1$.

NOTES

1. Corrected ordinary least squares are typically used to estimate deterministic frontiers in cross-sectional data. This procedure was explained by Greene: http://pages.stern.nyu.edu/~wgreene/FrontierModeling/SurveyPapers/Greene-FRONTIERS.pdf.
2. This is a typical procedure to clean data for outlier observations.

REFERENCES

Escolano, J., L. Jaramillo, C. Mulas-Granados, and G. Terrier. 2014. "How Much Is a Lot? Historical Evidence on the Size of Fiscal Adjustments." IMF Working Paper 14/179, International Monetary Fund, Washington, DC.

Herrera, S., and E. Munoz. 2019. "What Determines the Size of Public Employment? An Empirical Investigation." Background Report for Regional Study on Budget Rigidities in Latin America, unpublished paper, World Bank, Washington, DC.

Herrera, S., and J. Velasco. 2019. "Budget Rigidity in LAC: A Proposed New Measure for Empirical Analysis." Background Report for Regional Study on Budget Rigidities in Latin America, unpublished paper, World Bank, Washington, DC.

Muñoz, Erico, and Eduardo Olaberria. 2019. "Are Budget Rigidities a Source of Fiscal Distress and a Constraint for Fiscal Consolidation?" Background Report for Regional Study on Budget Rigidities in Latin America, unpublished paper, World Bank, Washington, DC.